MORE
love,
MORE
joy!

Judy,
Wishing you
More love & more joy!
Blessings,
Ryan

MORE love, MORE joy!

Simple Steps to Improve Your Relationships & Your Life

JENNIFER MARTIN & RYAN WEST

Discovery Bay Books
Port Townsend, WA

Discovery Bay Books
2023 E. Sims Way #275
Port Townsend, WA 98368
www.DiscoveryBayBooks.com

Copyright © 2007 Jennifer Martin and Ryan West

All rights reserved. No part of this publication may be reproduced in whole or in part, stored in a retrieval system, or transmitted in any form or by any means electronic, mechanical, photocopying, recording, or otherwise without the written permission of the publisher.

More Love, More Joy! is a trademark of Discovery Bay Productions, LLC.

Most Discovery Bay Books titles are available at special rates for sales promotions, premiums, fundraising, or educational use. Volume discounts and bulk purchases are offered for qualified buyers. Contact the Special Markets Department at Discovery Bay Books 1-800-936-0036.

Names have been changed to respect the privacy of those whose stories have been told in this book.

Disclaimers:
The purpose of this book is to educate and entertain. The publisher and authors are not licensed psychotherapists and are not offering psychiatric, psychological, or therapeutic care. This book and its contents are not intended to substitute or replace professional psychological advice, diagnosis, care, or treatment. If you have questions or concerns regarding psychological or emotional issues, whether about a relationship or otherwise, please be advised to consult with a licensed mental healthcare provider immediately for accurate diagnosis and treatment.

The authors, publishers, and their agents are not responsible for any injury or claim arising from the promotion, participation, organization, or hosting of any *More Love, More Joy!* Circles or peer-hosted groups. Organizing or participating in such an event is done entirely at each individual's own risk.

First Edition October 2007
Cover, text design, and illustrations by Ryan West
Copyediting by Winifred Sanchez

Publisher's Cataloging-in-Publication Data

Martin, Jennifer, 1963-
   More love, more joy! : simple steps to improve your relationships & your life / Jennifer Martin & Ryan West. -- 1st ed.
     p. cm.
     Includes index.
     LCCN 2007906017
     ISBN-13: 978-1-934681-22-0
     ISBN-10: 1-934681-22-9

     1. Love. 2. Intimacy (Psychology) 3. Interpersonal relations. I. West, Ryan. II. Title.

BF575.L8M37 2007   158.2
                        QBI07-600257

Contents

Acknowledgements	9
Introduction	11
CHAPTER 1: Getting Started	**15**
About the Process	17
Part 1: Making Room for More Love	18
Part 2: Your Wishbook	19
Part 3: Learn How to Ask for What You Want	19
What You'll Need to Get Started	20
How to Work the Process	20
The Major Elements of this Book	21
Are You in a Relationship Now?	23
Completing *More Love, More Joy!* as Part of a Circle/Group	23
Circle Guidelines	24
CHAPTER 2: Identifying Your Priorities	**27**
Exercise 1: Love Life Inventory	30
Exercise 2: What is Your Highest Priority?	32
Exercise 3: What's Your Motivation?	33
Exercise 4: What's Holding You Back?	35
The Importance of Communication	37
Keeping Your Audience Listening	37
Communication Tips	37
Tone of Voice	37
Misunderstood Messages	38
Asking for Help	39
Exercise 5: Asking for Help	40
Exercise 6: Decide How You Will Stay Motivated	40
Tip of the Week	41

CHAPTER 3: Opening the Door to More Love — 43
Meditation: Clean Slate 45
Exercise 1: I am, I have, I know how to 50
Exercise 2: Tooting Your Own Horn 52
Choosing to be Happy 53
Communication Tips 54
    Using "I Feel" Messages 54
    Show a Little Self-Respect 55
Exercise 3: Self-Talk and Self-Respect 55
Exercise 4: Discover Your Own Supportive Affirmations 56
Exercise 5: What is Your "Something Wonderful?" 57
Exercise 6: Contract to Care for Yourself with Love 58
Make Your Weekly Commitment 61
Tip of the Week 61

CHAPTER 4: What Have You Learned About Love? — 63
Exercise 1: What Did You Learn About Romantic Love? 65
Exercise 2: What Did You Learn About Self-Love? 67
Circle Exercise 3: Discussion 69
Meditation: Releasing Other's Rules About Love 70
Exercise 4: Create Your New "Love Rules" 73
Communication Tips 74
    The Power of Acknowledging 74
    Honoring Your Boundaries & Saying "No" 75
    How to Say "No" 75
    Keep Your "But" to Yourself 76
    Diplomatically & Respectfully Disagreeing 77
Exercise 5: Just Say "No" 76
Exercise 6: Disagreeing Using the Conjunction "And" 78
Exercise 7: Affirmations 78
Exercise 8: Bless & Release Your Love Role Models (optional) .. 79
Exercise 9: Flush & Release (optional) 79
Make Your Weekly Commitments 79
Tip of the Week 79

CHAPTER 5: Forgiveness & Letting Go of the Past — 81
Exercise 1: Would You Like to Forgive Yourself? 83
Meditation: Self-Forgiveness 83

Exercise 2: Your Dream Team 87
Self-Forgiveness Ritual 89
My Boyfriend Carl 89
Releasing Our Connection 90
A Karma Primer 92
Exercise 3: Releasing an Emotionally Charged Relationship 93
An Overview of Releasing an Emotionally Charged Relationship ... 94
Karmic Release Contract 95
Communication Tips 96
    The Value of a Balanced Apology 96
    Preparing to Ask for Forgiveness 96
    How to Apologize 97
    How to Receive an Apology 98
Exercise 4: Saying "I'm Sorry" 100
Exercise 5: Forgiveness Affirmations 100
Make Your Weekly Commitments 101
Tip of the Week 101

CHAPTER 6: Learning to Honor Receiving   103

Learning to Receive 105
The Cycle of Giving and Receiving 106
Accepting Generosity 108
Exercise 1: Create Your Receiving Log 109
The Transformation: Learning to Receive Continued 109
Communication Tips 111
    Show Your Appreciation 111
    Being a Good Receiver 111
Exercise 2: Saying "Thank You" 112
Universal Balance and Equal Exchange 112
Meditation: The Cycle of Giving & Receiving 113
Exercise 3: Create a Visual Reminder to Honor Receiving 117
Exercise 4: Affirmations to Honor Receiving 117
Make Your Weekly Commitments 117
Tip of the Week 117

CHAPTER 7: Creating a Life You'll Love   119

How a Fortune Cookie Changed My Life 120
Exercise 1: Create Your Own Fortune 122

The Power of Intentions 124
Exercise 2: Stating Your Intentions 125
Meditation: Letting Go of Limiting Beliefs 126
Your Words Create Your Reality 129
Take Your Intentions to the World 131
Connecting to What You Want 132
Miracle Networking 133
Make Your Weekly Commitments 133
Tip of the Week 133
Miracle Networking Gathering 134

CHAPTER 8: Discovering Your Desires & Building Your Wishbook 137
Make Your Weekly Commitments 139
Tip of the Week 139
Exercise 1: Make Your Personal Wishbook 139
Exercise 2: Create Your Body Pleasure Map 160

CHAPTER 9: Asking for What You Want 167
Exercise 1: Identifying Your Growth 167
Asking for What You Want 168
Communication Tips 169
    Before an Important Conversation 169
    Asking for Your Wishes Using the "I Love You Sandwich". 169
Exercise 2: Practice Using the "I Love You Sandwich". 171
More Communication Tips 173
    Introducing Your Wishbook to Your Partner 173
    If Your Wishbook Talk Needs a Little Extra Boost, WIIFM! 174
Exercise 3: Sharing Your Wishbook 175
Choice & Compromise 175
Circle Exercise 4: Share Your Admiration 177
And So You Have Come to the End 177
Please Keep in Touch 179

Our Credo 180

Index 181

About the Authors 191

Acknowledgements

There are a few people who have contributed greatly to the creation of this book, the meditation CD, and our seminars who deserve their angel wings. Patiently they supported us as the title of the book evolved, the format was set, the chapters grew, shrank, and grew again, and the entire process took on a life of its own.

Ten thousand thank yous to Marilyn May, for holding the light and actively participating in so many ways to bring *More Love, More Joy!* to the world. Special thanks also go out to our many friends and supporters for sharing their wisdom and insight during the book's evolution. In alphabetical order we'd like to particularly send our appreciation to: Carol Ellis, Linda Kardos, Sue Jenkins, Dee Ruzicka, and Bonnie Whyte, who each dramatically impacted the direction of this book. Big hugs and thank you's also go out to our test readers for their time spent scrutinizing every detail of the original manuscript and most importantly, their honesty: this list includes everyone already mentioned as well as Pati Beaudoin, Judy Dahl, Sue Detienne, Rhonda Hull, Anne Langendorfer, John McFadden, Liza Patchen-Short, and Megan Ziskovsky. To our copyeditor, Winifred Sanchez, thank you for pointing us in the right direction. And lastly, we wish to extend our appreciation to our families for their love and unconditional support.

Introduction

"Where there is love there is life."
~ Mahatma Gandhi

When I was younger, it seemed that I was always the person my friends, acquaintances, and colleagues came to talk with when something in their lives wasn't working. I remember when a friend of mine, Karen,* was complaining about Michael, her soon to be husband. She told me she was on the verge of divorce and she hadn't even gotten married yet.

Karen's 25th birthday had just passed. She had hoped that Michael would have surprised her with a big party. Since Michael knew that Karen loved jewelry (or so she thought), she hoped he would have given her a special necklace for her gift. She knew exactly what she wanted and was pretty sure that he did, too.

But on the day of her birthday, nothing happened. In fact, Michael called to say that he was working late. When Karen realized that this wasn't a ploy to give her a surprise party, she was fuming. The next day, Michael went back to work and still hadn't acknowledged Karen's birthday. He had obviously forgotten.

That night when Michael came home, he gave Karen a birthday card. This wasn't the first time Michael was so lost in his own world that he had forgotten something Karen felt was important. Karen had had enough. How could she marry such a jerk?

*Names have been changed.

I patiently listened to Karen's story. When she had finished, I asked if Michael really knew about Karen's desires. I mean, did he know exactly what she wanted: a necklace, a cake, a big surprise party? And then she realized, regardless of how many times she might have hinted, she had never specifically requested these things.

When I talked to Karen more about what had prevented her from asking directly for what she wanted, she recognized that there were many things holding her back. On some level, she believed it was too late to ask, that she'd never get what she wanted, and that she wouldn't even know where to start or what to say. And then she came to the one concept that stood out more than all the others; asking for what she wanted would be selfish, "wouldn't it?"

I suspected that if Karen wasn't getting her needs met, there was a good chance that Michael wasn't either. When I asked her about this, Karen couldn't really say for certain if she was 100% on target with regard to how she cared for her fiancé. She said that although she and Michael spoke all the time, talking about how their needs might be changing was never really a topic of conversation. When I asked why this wasn't a priority, my question was answered with another laundry list of excuses. It was clear to me that the issue went much deeper, and I suspected that Karen wasn't the only one in this position.

Discovering the Common Denominator

When I asked around, I quickly learned that many people shared Karen's frustrations. Some people recognized that they didn't know what they wanted, one couple wondered how it would be possible to break long-standing patterns in their relationship, and a few admitted that they lacked the courage to ask for what they desired. One man said he was so tired of getting it wrong when he attempted to do something nice for his wife that he stopped trying altogether. And then finally one woman shared an answer that really made the most sense: "I can't put my finger on it, but something inside me is holding me back." She definitely was on to something.

The truth is, sometimes, whether we are aware of it or not, our past can get in the way of our present or our future. Regardless of your experience, even if you feel that everything is great in your life, you might unconsciously be preventing yourself from reaching your true potential in life and in love.

I knew from both my personal experiences and those of my clients that transforming these unknown obstacles doesn't have to be difficult. Many times, making small changes like using different words in the way you communicate with yourself, or cutting the ties to something you don't want anymore, can create profound differences in your life. There is no reason you cannot have both a life you love and when and if you are ready, a love life that makes you happy. All you may need to do is learn how to get out of your own way.

Getting Out of My Own Way

When I first had the idea of writing *More Love, More Joy!*, I heard a little voice inside me ask, "What makes you qualified to write this book?" Somehow it didn't seem to matter that I already had a very clear concept for the text, a history of helping people get more of what they wanted, and a 9-year-old love relationship based on respect, balance, acceptance, and equal exchange. Despite my background, I knew that some people might still wonder about my qualifications since I wasn't an official love doctor, just a love cheerleader.

I eventually came to the realization that regardless of my formal training, I was passionate about this process. I knew from my own experience just how well it works. Over and over, I kept hearing from friends and clients about how much they needed this book. With their encouragement, I decided to forge ahead.

So who am I? I'm a regular person who, just like you, has had to figure out how to create healthy, satisfying relationships on my own. I've made mistakes, stubbed my toes, and along the way learned some incredibly valuable lessons. I would be lying if I said I have figured everything out or didn't have anything left to learn. Like most people, I continue to grow and evolve every day.

In my experience as a personal coach, certified hypnotherapist, and business development consultant, my own communication and relationship theories have been developed and put to the test. The result is *More Love, More Joy!*, a culmination of tried and true tools and strategies that have been successfully implemented in my own life and the lives of my clients, friends, family, acquaintances, and colleagues.

Since the stories and many of the processes are my own, you will find that the text has been primarily written in the first person. However, this book has been a collaborative effort with my co-author, Ryan West. Without Ryan's contributions and support, *More Love, More Joy!* would never have evolved to what it is now.

Whether or not you are in a love relationship, know what you want, believe you deserve to have it, or even have the courage to ask, *More Love, More Joy!* can light the way. My dream is that you find something within these pages or in a *More Love, More Joy!* Circle or Seminar that reminds you that you are worthy of being loved for the unique individual you are, in exactly the way you desire.

Bless you for coming to know yourself and learning how to ask specifically for what you want from those who love you.

Enjoy the journey.

– Jennifer Martin

Editorial Notes:
Throughout this book you'll find we have adopted the word "Partner" to reference husbands, wives, girlfriends, and boyfriends, significant others, lovers, sweethearts, and any other pet names you might have for the one you love. With regards to gender, as grammatically incorrect as it may be, we have used "they" or "their," in place of "he or she" or "his or her" throughout the text. We hope you will mentally replace these references with words that feel appropriate for you personally.

1

Getting Started

"Love yourself, trust your choices, and everything is possible."
~ Cherie Carter-Scott

If you imagine the most wonderful night out, what would it be? Dinner at a quiet romantic restaurant? Going out with friends to a dance club or favorite bar? Anything, just so long as you didn't have to cook or be Mommy or Daddy for a night?

Now what if, as if by magic, your current or future husband or wife, boyfriend or girlfriend knew exactly what this incredible night out included. Even better, the next time they wanted to do something nice for you, they planned and executed this dream date without even having to ask.

Believe it or not, this scenario doesn't have to be too good to be true. If you are still waiting to be surprised with that perfect night out, if you've struggled with explaining your needs or desires to your partner, or if you have ever wondered what you can do to improve your relationships, *More Love, More Joy!* can help.

If you are ready to participate in creating your own happiness, want to learn more about yourself, or wish to experience more mutually fulfilling love relationships, this book includes inspiring stories, practical strategies, and step-by-step exercises that can help you take

> ### *More Love, More Joy!* can help . . .
>
> **You:**
> - Identify what makes you feel happy
> - Learn to effectively ask for what you want
> - Let go of anything that may be blocking your ability to experience the most fulfilling love life possible
> - Improve communication in every area of your life
>
> **Your Partner:**
> - Understand you and how to fulfill your wants and needs better than ever before
> - Learn specific ways to please you that don't involve mind-reading, guessing, or the stress of potentially being wrong
>
> **Both of You:**
> - Increase intimacy
> - Enhance the love and joy in your relationship
> - Bring more balance to your relationship
> - Develop mutual respect and understanding

positive steps toward your goals.

It is never too late to be happy. I don't care if you are 18 or 80, gay or straight, single or in a relationship, both you and your partner can have more love and joy in your lives.

The primary focus of this journey is on love. Loving yourself, your partner, and your life. Although the priority here may be on bringing *you* more of what *you* want, asking to be cared for in the way you wish is not a shallow and self-centered idea; it's a practical one. By overcoming your own obstacles, learning to communicate your desires, and honoring your own boundaries, you can create longer-lasting and more mutually satisfying relationships (either already existing or new).

Asking your partner for what you truly want can actually take you to the core of a deeper, ever-evolving love relationship. When you both are able to share your needs and desires openly, you have the opportunity to honor your authentic self as well as the inner spirit of your partner. At an even higher level, the more deeply and authentically you connect with one another, the more you magnify your capacity to share love with each other and the world around you.

About the Process

More Love, More Joy! is comprised of three parts to be completed over an 8-week period, all essential to helping you create the type of love relationship you've always wanted:

1. First you'll start by **Making Room for More Love** by learning how to quickly release old habits, patterns, and leftover baggage, thereby freeing yourself to enjoy the most satisfying love life possible. You'll also begin to explore communication techniques that will enhance your success in any conversation.

2. Next, you'll create **Your Wishbook**. This is a personalized instruction manual that includes specific directions for how to care for you in your own unique way.

3. And at the end, you'll practice techniques to introduce your Wishbook to your partner and learn how to **Ask for What You Want**.

Throughout the process, you'll be introduced to many concepts to help you communicate more successfully with others, including your partner. These tools can enhance your ability to understand each other more clearly and help you experience love in the ways you both desire.

Regardless of how long you may have been in your current relationship or the length of time you might have been doing things the old way, this complete process can help you discover more about yourself and your partner, even if only one of you does the work. If you are single, the techniques in this book will still bring you value. These exercises can help you begin to develop (or improve upon) a strong personal foundation, while increasing your self-awareness and strengthening your commitment to self-love and care. You'll walk away from this process with a greater sense of clarity and the communication tools that can assist you in any relationship.

Part 1: Making Room for More Love

As you begin to open yourself to the most fulfilling love life possible, you will find that much of this book is dedicated to helping you release anything that may be holding you back from experiencing the love you want. Consider this portion (Chapters 1-7), the opportunity to clean, de-clutter, and organize your "love closet" (the place that stores everything that effects how you experience love). This is your chance to identify the good, toss out anything you don't want, and make room for the new. You'll explore a variety of tools that can help you broaden your perspective, lighten your load, and expand your potential for love. Everything is explained in practical, step-by-step details to ensure your success.

Because everyone's personal issues and priorities are different, you will begin by identifying areas of your current relationship (or last meaningful relationship if you are single) that you would like to focus on improving. You'll have ample opportunities to address your highest priorities right from the start by implementing communication strategies and other techniques found in every chapter.

A broad range of topics will prepare you to experience the most fulfilling love life possible:

- You'll learn how to unlock your capacity for love by letting go of other people's limiting perceptions of who or what you are, while learning to be more loving to yourself.

- You'll have a chance to consider the "Love Rules" you've inherited from your role models. You'll then be able to honor what worked and release anything you don't want to keep.

- You'll be given an opportunity to let go of limiting beliefs and any old relationships that might be holding you back, once and for all.

- You'll discover how learning to honor receiving can bring more balance into your life, which completes the cycle of reciprocal love.

- You'll practice creating the life (and love) you want by acting from your intentions in alignment with what is in the highest and best good for all.

These preliminary steps will help you move beyond the past and make room for more love and joy in your relationship(s). And, the best news is that doing this process can be fun, whether you complete it on your own, with a partner, or as a part of a *More Love, More Joy!* Circle.[*]

Part 2: Your Wishbook

Have you ever secretly hoped that your partner would just listen to you blow off steam following a difficult situation rather than trying to solve your problems? Or maybe after a tough day, have you ever wanted to be by yourself for awhile instead of being pushed to talk about it?

Unfortunately, since we didn't all come automatically programmed to share with others how we want them to care for us, asking for what we *really* want sometimes presents a challenge. Most of our partners really do want to please us, but sometimes they just don't know how. Regardless of how hard they try, even the most loving and well-intended people can't always read each other's minds.

Creating your Wishbook can be the solution to these problems. Your Wishbook is your personal instruction manual that can provide your partner with detailed specifics about how to please you. It can help eliminate ambiguity about major issues, whether you're starting a new relationship or working to enhance the one you are already in.

If you've ever had trouble (or never considered) sharing with your partner what you'd really like for your anniversary, how to support you when you're feeling sad, or how to satisfy you even more in the bedroom, your Wishbook will cover all this and much more. Creating your Wishbook is easy, and it can be invaluable to your relationship, too.

Part 3: Learn How to Ask for What You Want

Once you've completed your Wishbook, you can use it to help you and your partner learn and understand more about each other. Then you'll have an easy way to (re)open the door to better communication. This can present a great opportunity to create or recreate your lives together

---

[*]Learn more about *More Love, More Joy!* Circles on page 23.

as you both wish. In Chapter 9, you'll discover techniques to prepare for important conversations and learn how to phrase your requests in a way that will allow your partner to stay receptive, listening, and excited to learn more. This can be a magnificent opportunity to broaden your perspectives and enhance the way you love. Are you ready?

What You'll Need to Get Started

1. A Special Journal or Notebook
2. A Pen or Pencil
3. (Optional) CD Player for Recorded Meditations*
4. **An Open Mind:** You'll be trying things that may be new to you. Openness is essential to getting the most out of the process.
5. **A Commitment to Treat Yourself Kindly:** Actively practicing self-love is fundamental to *More Love, More Joy!* If you experience some growing pains during your exploration, remember that this is a perfect time to practice being gentle with yourself. Give yourself as much time as you need to go through the process. Schedule some personal time each week just for you!

*More Love, More Joy! Meditations (sold separately) are a recorded collection of the meditations in this book. Just pop in the CD, select the track, and get ready to relax!

How to Work the Process

Whether you are working on your own, with a partner, or as a part of a Circle, I encourage you to pace yourself. Please give every aspect of your journey and the discovery of your personal Wishbook ample time to unfold and develop. Don't try to take on the entire process all at once. I suggest you complete no more than one chapter per week, finishing each of the chapters and their contents in chronological order. Once you begin working on your Wishbook in Chapter 8, feel free to go as quickly or leisurely as you wish.

Chapters 2 through 7 are the foundation of this course. You may find that completing this work prior to writing your Wishbook can be both empowering and helpful. Often, those who complete the preliminary work are able to more fully experience the changes they desire in their lives than those who just jump directly to the creation of their personal Wishbook.

However, we recognize that each person is unique. Reading every chapter and trying every exercise just won't be right for everyone. If you find yourself bored or having real difficulty completing any exercise or assignment within a particular week, honor those feelings. Please don't give up on the whole process, just skip ahead to the next exercise or chapter that captures your interest or that you feel would be helpful.

The Major Elements of this Book

You will find that there are many components to the *More Love, More Joy!* process. The following are some main elements and suggestions for how to use each one.

The Credo

The foundational beliefs and goals of this work are outlined in the Credo, found on page 180. We use this statement as a way to connect each of us in common beliefs and purpose. All *More Love, More Joy!* peer-hosted Circle meetings (groups) begin by speaking the Credo aloud.

Meditations

Also included are guided visualizations we call "meditations" that can help you relax and let go of things that no longer serve you. If you aren't familiar with this type of exercise, you simply listen to a story with your eyes closed. As you relax, you experience your own version of the story in your mind. It can be a very empowering way to explore possibilities and help you create the changes that you desire.

The easiest way to do the meditations is to listen to the recorded CD.[*] If you are doing the work by yourself, this CD will make it easier

[*] For information about the Meditation CD visit our website, www.MoreLoveMoreJoy.com, or see page 187.

for you to enjoy all of the components of this book. Alternatively, if you are doing this work with a partner or as part of a Circle, one person can read the meditation to the other(s).

Affirmations
An affirmation is a simple statement that reinforces your intention to create or enhance something in your life. These phrases are stated in the positive and can include emotions, states of mind, and tangible or physical desires. Using affirmations can be a simple and effective way to participate in bringing your dreams to life.

Communication Tips
You will find exercises and suggestions in each chapter that can help you ask for (and often receive) more of what you want in your love relationships and in every aspect of your life. Put them into action and watch your communication skills improve throughout this process.

Exercises
Each chapter includes a variety of exercises to help you (re)discover your core essence and enhance your belief that you can receive love in the unique way that you wish. There are journal questions, lists to consider, and step-by-step instructions to help you create the changes you desire in your life.

Circle Exercises & Notes
It is important to mention that although you can successfully work this process on your own, there are a few exercises included in the book that were created specifically to be done in pairs or as a group. You will find grey boxes on the left-hand page at the start of every chapter that indicate how to prepare for your next Circle if you are participating in a group. Exercises specific to Circles are also noted as such. Read more about Circles on the next page.

Are You in a Relationship Now?

If you have the luxury of being in a relationship with someone who is open and committed to the growth and evolution of your partnership, we suggest that each of you complete this entire book. However, you will still find great value in this process even if only one of you does the work or if the two of you just complete and then share your answers to the questions in the Wishbook (Chapter 8). There are many ways to approach doing this book with your partner. We encourage you to discover the methods that feel most comfortable for both of you.

If you are doing *More Love, More Joy!* together, please practice being kind with yourselves and one another during this process. Remember to be patient and willing to compromise a little. If you experience any bumps in the road, know they are only temporary. Stick with it, and remember, the best may be yet to come!

Completing *More Love, More Joy!* as Part of a Circle/Group

This work can be done by yourself or with your honey and can be absolutely incredible and life changing. However, there are two great benefits to completing this process in a group, or "Circle." First, it can be a perfect way to build community and connect with supportive friends. Secondly, people tend to be more accountable to strangers, so they end up getting more accomplished with peer support. You may have experienced this in your own life. If you have a commitment to a peer group to get your homework done by a certain day every week, you probably are less likely to let it get pushed aside by something else in your life. In short, each member has a better chance of reaching individual success as a part of a *More Love, More Joy!* Circle.

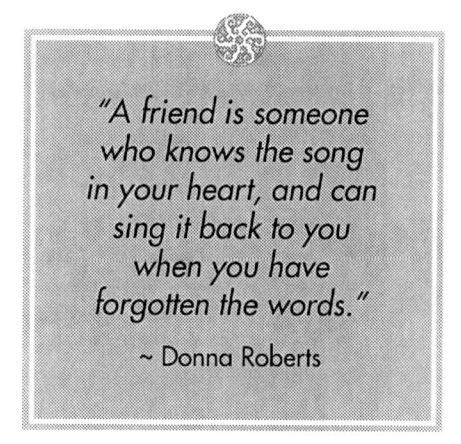

> *"A friend is someone who knows the song in your heart, and can sing it back to you when you have forgotten the words."*
>
> ~ Donna Roberts

This book fully supports group work. You'll notice at the beginning of each chapter (after Chapter 1) that there is an indication of what work should be completed individually as homework before you arrive at your weekly meeting. On that note, we have created this work as an 8-week process. However, your group can alternatively meet biweekly or monthly.

If you'd like to join a peer-hosted Circle, check our website, www.MoreLoveMoreJoy.com, for a list of upcoming groups and their start dates. If you can't locate one in your area or you want to start a Circle of your own, we'll provide you with everything you'll need to get started. On our website you'll find free downloadable posters, invitations, answers to frequently asked questions, outlines for what to do at each gathering, and group discounts on books and other materials.

Hosting your own Circle is easy doesn't require any special training. Anyone can have great success hosting a group by using this book in conjunction with the start-up instructions, weekly outlines, and other resources we provide. Invite your friends, family, and neighbors and create a supportive community. For more information visit us online.

Circle Guidelines

Dear Circle Hosts and Members:

You will find that part of the *More Love, More Joy!* process is about asking to be treated and loved in the ways that you desire. As the authors of this material, we would like to ask you to follow these guidelines along with those on our website. Thank you for respecting and honoring our requests.

1. Please adhere to the guidelines set forth in the book and on the website. Everyone in a Circle, including the Host, is expected to participate in the process, do the homework, and share as part of the group. Please do

CONTINUED ▶

not add anything (chanting, drumming, psychotherapy or related modalities, etc.) to the meetings without our written authorization.

2. We ask that if you advertise or promote your gathering that you use the posters, invitations, and other endorsed marketing materials that we provide for free on our website. It is important that the *More Love, More Joy!* message is communicated consistently. Also, using the materials and information we provide can make attracting others to your Circle that much easier.

3. Ideally, our wish is to support peer-led Circles that are free of charge. Because *More Love, More Joy!* does not certify or train Circle Hosts, we hope that the savings are passed onto Circle members. If a fee needs to be charged, we encourage the Host to offer a sliding scale fee or to allow members to make a "love offering" donation so that everyone interested can join.

4. We ask that each Circle member purchase her or his own book. Volume discount prices for groups are available directly from the website/publisher. Please do not duplicate or record any part of our copyrighted materials (books, CD's, etc.) without our expressed written permission.

5. We always try to keep updated postings of all upcoming groups on our website. Please register your Circle at www.MoreLoveMoreJoy.com at least 3 weeks prior to your start date. That way, we can direct anyone interested in joining your group right to you.

6. Lastly, we ask for Circle members and Hosts to keep in touch with us. We love hearing about your successes and how you enjoyed the process.

We hope that you are inspired to recreate your life in whatever ways bring you more pleasure. Enjoy the journey!

FOR CIRCLE MEMBERS

Complete prior to attending your 1st Circle

Week 1 Homework:
- Read Intro
- Read Chapter 1
- Read Chapter 2
- Do Exercises 5 & 6

Bring to the Meeting:
- Your *More Love, More Joy!* book
- A journal/notebook and a pen/pencil

In Your Circle You Will Complete:
- Exercises 1-4

2

Identifying Your Priorities

"The first step to getting the things you want out of life is this: Decide what you want."
~ Ben Stein

Max got married at 22. "That was what we did in my day," he would tell you, "We found a gal and tied the knot." Max thought Carol was "a good catch." He was determined to make her his wife.

Carol had a kind face and a loving heart. Once they were married, she cooked and cleaned their tiny apartment and later the house they bought on Champion Road. "It's a sign," she said when they found the house, telling Max she knew that he was a champion. She was sure he could accomplish anything he set his mind to doing.

The years passed more or less pleasantly until one morning, shortly after their 37th anniversary, Max woke up in a panic. He realized he felt lost. He couldn't remember the last time he and Carol shared anything close to "romance." Heck, in the last 5 years or so they had barely even shared a meal. Once the kids had grown and left home, the couple had developed their own independent lives. On that morning, Max became vibrantly aware that he wanted something different. He just wasn't quite sure what that something different was.

While lying in bed, Max pondered the options. As much as he thought he could just as easily move on, the truth was that he loved

Carol. He just didn't know who she was anymore. She had been a great mother to their children and had taken good care of him all these years. He missed feeling like he was invincible. He missed his cheerleader. He envied the young couples who held hands and always seemed to be noticeably in love. Was it too late to feel that way?

On the way into work that morning, Max called his sister, Fran. Max knew Franny understood women. She would know what he should do. She told Max, "It is never too late if two people truly love each other." She believed a couple could find that romantic spark again if they were both courageous enough to try.

> *"You are never given a wish without also being given the power to make it true."*
>
> ~ Richard Bach

By the end of their conversation, Max was determined to get to know his wife all over again. Franny suggested that Max start with something small and convinced him to talk to Carol. As much as it might not be easy for him, Franny knew that Carol would respond to hearing Max tell her how he really felt. What woman wouldn't want to hear that she was loved and desired?

That evening, Max found Carol in front of the television. He didn't know where to start, but he managed to let her know that he felt like they didn't really know each other any more. Then he told her something that she hadn't heard in too many years, "I love you."

Max shared with Carol that he couldn't remember when they started to move down different paths, but, "I want to be your husband again." Then Max gathered his courage and asked Carol out for a date. It didn't take long before Carol started crying. She had given up on love and romance a long time ago, and now it seemed her champion had returned.

Your Journey

Regardless of your age or where you are in your life, there is always the potential to have more of what you want, even if, like Max, you don't know exactly what that is. Sometimes, just taking that first courageous step to ask for something different can lead to a great victory.

There is no better time than right now to start living your life in a way that brings you more joy, happiness, and laughter, lots of it. Just imagine the possibilities!

This process can be extremely gratifying and can take your relationships to the next level. It doesn't matter how long you may have been with your current partner or the quality of your relationships in the past. You will find this work can help you change your personal approach to love. Sometimes, just looking at something in a different way or adopting a new attitude is all that is needed for you and your partner to experience a more mutually satisfying relationship together.

Completing this process can be graceful and easy. Along the way, keep in mind that as you are creating the love life you truly desire, your changes and requests may be in alignment with what your current or future partner wants, too. While doing the work, try to give yourself time to both complete assignments and assimilate what you are learning. The end result can be better than anything that you've ever imagined.

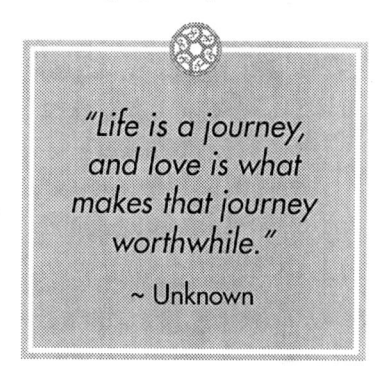

> "Life is a journey, and love is what makes that journey worthwhile."
>
> ~ Unknown

Throughout this chapter, you'll discover what your goals are and why you are doing this work. Take your time, be gentle with yourself, and know that this can be your chance for a new beginning. No matter what your past has included, this is your opportunity to experience more love and joy in your everyday life.

EXERCISE 1: Love Life Inventory

This exercise will give you a chance to take an honest look at either your current partnership or your most recent meaningful relationship. Your responses will provide a baseline as you move forward in this process.

1. Begin by reading through all the categories of the Love Life Inventory on the following page before answering.

2. As you look over each subject, consider how you feel about this category as it relates to your relationship.

    For Example:

    When you review the section titled "Birthdays and Anniversaries," think of all the ways that these special days play into your relationship. Think of what you would like to do on these days and what you have experienced with your partner in the past. Have you received gifts that reflected what you wanted? Did you feel you were treated with the respect or appreciation (or anything else) that you would've liked from your partner? Did your partner respond to your desires in the ways you wished?

3. Consider all the aspects relating to each different category. Whatever thoughts come to mind, first rate your relationship on a scale of 1-10 (10 being best) relating to where it is now (or if you're single, where it was in your last meaningful relationship). Next, circle a number relating to what you would like it to be, your goal. Keep in mind that not everyone is looking for a 10 for every category and that's okay.

4. Continue on down the list until you have completed all the categories. If there are other areas of your life that are important to you that haven't been included in this inventory, add your own categories using the additional spaces provided.

Love Life Inventory

Category	How does this rate?	What is your goal?
Birthdays & Anniversaries	1 2 3 4 5 6 7 8 9 10	1 2 3 4 5 6 7 8 9 10
Personal Time	1 2 3 4 5 6 7 8 9 10	1 2 3 4 5 6 7 8 9 10
Shared Time	1 2 3 4 5 6 7 8 9 10	1 2 3 4 5 6 7 8 9 10
Responsibilities & Chores	1 2 3 4 5 6 7 8 9 10	1 2 3 4 5 6 7 8 9 10
Hobbies & Travel	1 2 3 4 5 6 7 8 9 10	1 2 3 4 5 6 7 8 9 10
Money & Finances	1 2 3 4 5 6 7 8 9 10	1 2 3 4 5 6 7 8 9 10
Religion/Spirituality	1 2 3 4 5 6 7 8 9 10	1 2 3 4 5 6 7 8 9 10
Romance	1 2 3 4 5 6 7 8 9 10	1 2 3 4 5 6 7 8 9 10
Intimacy	1 2 3 4 5 6 7 8 9 10	1 2 3 4 5 6 7 8 9 10
Sex	1 2 3 4 5 6 7 8 9 10	1 2 3 4 5 6 7 8 9 10
Communication	1 2 3 4 5 6 7 8 9 10	1 2 3 4 5 6 7 8 9 10
Immediate Family	1 2 3 4 5 6 7 8 9 10	1 2 3 4 5 6 7 8 9 10
Extended Family	1 2 3 4 5 6 7 8 9 10	1 2 3 4 5 6 7 8 9 10
Friends	1 2 3 4 5 6 7 8 9 10	1 2 3 4 5 6 7 8 9 10
Other _____	1 2 3 4 5 6 7 8 9 10	1 2 3 4 5 6 7 8 9 10
Other _____	1 2 3 4 5 6 7 8 9 10	1 2 3 4 5 6 7 8 9 10

EXERCISE 2: What is Your Highest Priority?

Congratulations! You have completed the first step in identifying some areas within your relationship that can be improved. Now let's figure out the most important areas to focus your attention.

1. **Choose Your Top Two Priorities**

    Take another look through your inventory. You'll already be working on the Communication category throughout this book. So, consider which two categories (other than Communication) you feel would impact your enjoyment of your (current or future) relationships most if they were to change for the better.

    Note: If you are single, you may want to choose categories that are immediately relevant to your life. Creating change now can positively impact your future relationships.

2. **Explore the Possibilities & Determine Your Goals**

    Once you have made your choice, write your first category at the top of a journal page and your second category at the top of a second journal page. Under each heading, describe what would need to change for this category to reflect your goal number. Record any thoughts or feelings that come to mind.

    For Example:

    If you choose "Personal Time," maybe in order to take this area from a 5 to a 10 you could do this by having a special date to do something nice for yourself every week or by spending at least 30 minutes alone every evening.

3. **Create an Action List of Steps You'll Take to Overcome Your Challenges**

    How can you constructively move closer to what you'd ultimately like in your life? Be creative and think outside the box. Create your own Action List. Include at least four or five tangible steps you can take in the next few weeks to address each of your top priorities.

    For Example:

    If you want more "Shared Time," you might consider buying a Tivo® to record your TV shows so you wouldn't need to watch them on any set schedule. You could also take on fewer projects to make room in your life for your together time. Write down anything you think might help you overcome your relationship challenges and help you get more of what you want.

4. Your Weekly Commitment to Your Action List

Now that you have identified a few ways you can move towards your relationship goals, choose one item on your Action List to complete this week. Using the previous example, in the upcoming week you might buy and set up a Tivo® and plan your next date night together.

From this point forward, you will select a new step each week and put it into practice. This is your chance to continually address your highest priorities and actively improve your life. If at anytime during this process you complete all the items on your initial list, either brainstorm for more action steps or select a new category you'd like to improve and start working on a new list.

Keep Up the Good Work!

Have you heard the old joke, "How do you eat an elephant?" The answer is—"One bite at a time." Approach the *More Love, More Joy!* process in the same way. Each week we will guide you one step closer to your goal.

You are on the right track. Just keep taking those baby steps, and before you know it, you'll be getting more of what you want, not only from your partner, but in many areas of your life. Many of the same tips and tools we share with you throughout this book can be used with your boss, your parents or children, or even with the customer service person at the other end of the phone line. The more you focus on identifying what you want, the easier it can become to actually get it.

EXERCISE 3: What's Your Motivation?

Have you ever stayed at a job you didn't love or in a relationship that wasn't quite right for you much longer than you really wanted? Sometimes we have to recognize what doesn't work for us in order to feel motivated to make a change.

1. Take a look at some of the reasons that people have turned to this book. Check any answers that apply to you.

   I am doing this work because:

   ❑ I'm not getting everything I want in my relationship now.
   ❑ I'm on a quest to live my life more fully.
   ❑ I want to be a part of a relationship that continues to evolve and grow better and better all the time.
   ❑ I want to recapture a deep loving connection with my partner.
   ❑ I want to be happier in my (next or current) relationship.
   ❑ I've been compromising more than I really want.
   ❑ My relationship is good and I want great!
   ❑ Parts of my relationship work and others could be a lot better.
   ❑ I don't feel strong enough to stand up for what I want.
   ❑ I'm not sure if I know what I want anymore.
   ❑ I've forgotten who I am and what makes me happy.
   ❑ I know if my communication skills improve, my life will be better.
   ❑ I'd like to try everything I can to make my relationship work.
   ❑ It's been a long time since I talked with my partner about our lives together and I don't know where to start.
   ❑ My partner and I need to make some changes if our relationship is going to last.
   ❑ I would like to get to know my partner better.
   ❑ My self-esteem has left the building.
   ❑ I'm ready to find true love.

- ❏ I'm not the same as I used to be and I don't know how to tell my partner that I want something different than I did before.

- ❏ I really want to bring romance back into my life.

- ❏ I'm tired of being disappointed in my love life.

- ❏ I want to feel more sexually satisfied.

2. Now write in your journal any other ways that you could benefit from doing this work.

3. When you are done, take a look at the answers you've circled and anything you may have written. See if you can find two or three reasons that best sum up why you are doing this work. Write them on a separate 3 x 5 card or a piece of paper. If you find your commitment to the process waning, review your notes to help you remember your motivating factors for creating satisfying changes in your life.

EXERCISE 4: What's Holding You Back?

1. Check any of the following statements that you identify with personally. What might be preventing you from asking for what you really want, or what might have held you back in the past?

   - ❏ I'm not sure of what I want.

   - ❏ I don't know how to ask.

   - ❏ I've been stuck doing the same thing so long I don't know where to start.

   - ❏ I'm not sure I deserve it.

   - ❏ I feel trapped.

   - ❏ Asking would be out of character for me.

   - ❏ I wouldn't know what to say or how to say it.

   - ❏ I'm better at taking care of other people than I am at taking care of myself.

I'm afraid if I ask for what I want:
- ❏ I'd be rejected.
- ❏ I'd be embarrassed.
- ❏ I might not be respected.
- ❏ I might not get it.
- ❏ I'd be laughed at.
- ❏ I wouldn't be taken seriously.
- ❏ My partner could think I'm greedy or selfish.
- ❏ I'd be in personal conflict.

2. Is there anything else holding you back from asking for exactly what you want? Write down any other thoughts or feelings that come to mind.

3. Now imagine what your life might be like if you were able to let go of whatever might be holding you back. How could your life become more enjoyable? What would change for the better? Record your responses in your journal.

4. Finally, close your eyes. Imagine what this best version of your life FEELS like. Are you excited, energized, or filled with love? Whatever you feel, hold these thoughts and feelings in your mind and your body for as long as you can. When you are finished, write about what you experienced.

Beginning the Journey

When you want to create changes in your life, recognizing what you want is the first step. Have you discovered a few areas of your love life that you might want to enhance? Trust the process, be creative, and allow yourself room to get out of your own way.

Believing that you deserve to have what you want comes next. You'll have a chance to learn a little more about this in the next few chapters.

By the time you finish this book, you should be ready for the third step which is asking for the things you want. Don't worry if this hasn't been your strong point in the past. You'll have plenty of time to get used to the idea and several opportunities to practice so that you'll know just what to say when a situation presents itself.

The Importance of Communication

If there is one key that will unlock many doors, it is the way you speak to people. The words you use as well as when, how, and where you deliver them can impact your success in life dramatically. If I told you that fine tuning or improving your personal communication strategies could impact your love relationships and almost every area of your life, would you be open to learning a little more?

Keeping Your Audience Listening

Regardless of your message, it is imperative that the person you are speaking with stays open to hearing what you are saying during your conversation. Whatever you can do to maintain their interest and attention will ultimately help you reach your desired goals. You'll find many tips throughout this book that will support your success in this regard. Even if these ideas don't feel natural to you right away, I encourage you to continue using them as they can make a world of difference and help impact your success in creating the outcomes you seek.

COMMUNICATION TIPS

[TIP] Tone of Voice

The tone of your voice can have a great impact on your ability to influence others and simply be heard. What might sound like a regular tone to you may actually be turning off some listeners.

Have you ever noticed that when someone was yelling at you, you might not have heard exactly what they were saying? There are some things that trigger our fight or flight instincts and yelling can be one of them. When we perceive someone is raising their voice, we sometimes stop consciously listening while our minds begin figuring out how to escape. Keeping your voice at a moderate tone will help you get more of what you want because your audience can stay receptive and listening.

Now that we've talked about loud voices, conversely, if you speak very quietly, or the tone of your voice is very high or childlike, other people may interpret your tone as weak or insecure. Sometimes quiet voices can also convey to others that the person speaking doesn't believe in what they are saying.

You will have the most success asking for what you want if your tone of voice elicits confidence and conviction without being too soft, too loud, or too high pitched. This is one way you can keep your audience on-board and help them see that you are committed to your requests.

🆃🅸🅿 Misunderstood Messages

Sometimes the words we use mean one thing to us and something entirely different to the person with whom we are speaking. Can you remember a time when your partner or someone you cared about said something and you couldn't believe how insensitive or rude they were? Perhaps the message they intended wasn't quite what you heard.

Instead of assuming the worst, give the other person the benefit of the doubt if something they said felt unkind or confusing to you. If you find yourself in one of these sticky situations, first tell the other person you aren't sure if you understood them properly. If you are going to make an assumption, assume that they didn't intend to be mean or rude.

When you hear something that doesn't feel right, clarifying your understanding early on can help make things easier for your relationship in the long run. Share with the other person something like "what I just understood you said is . . .," while reiterating what you thought they said. This can give them the opportunity to confirm or clarify what they actually meant and prevent any unnecessary hard feelings.

Example Dialogue:

Heather: "Sharon, you are never going to find a husband if you don't let a guy feel like a man. Just because you are the president of your own company doesn't mean that you couldn't let a man take the lead sometimes."

Sharon: "Heather, maybe I didn't understand you. I thought I heard you say that 'I'll never get married if I don't lighten up and stop emasculating men.' Is that what you meant to say?"

Heather: "I'm sorry, I just meant that if you want to be in a relationship again, you might have better luck if you could remember that you don't always have to be in charge of everything. People like to be treated like equals in a relationship. Maybe you could let someone else be your co-pilot instead of you being the driver all the time. That's all."

Sharon: "Maybe you're right. I guess I just need to hold out for someone who is comfortable loving a strong woman like me. I think I'd be willing to back down a bit if I found a guy who could really carry his own weight. Thanks for being honest, I know you just want the best for me."

🆃🅸🅿 Asking for Help

Sometimes the best way to get what you want is to ask for help. And no, asking doesn't mean you are helpless or that you can't do something by yourself. As humans we are naturally inclined to lend a hand when someone asks for help. Therefore, if you reach out to ask for assistance, there is a good chance that you will get what you want. You may also give someone else a opportunity to feel good about being able to support you. Start your request by saying, "Can you help me?"

For Example:

- If you are tired of always making dinner, see if your partner can handle things once in awhile. Be willing to let them really take charge and make dinner their way. This might include going out to dinner or eating something you might not prepare yourself.

- When your flight has been cancelled or if your cell phone company has overbilled you, rather than raising your voice to the customer service representative and unloading all your frustrations, remember to keep your cool. You'll have far greater success if you start by asking, "Can you help me?"

EXERCISE 5: Asking for Help

This week, ask your partner or someone else for help with something small that you normally wouldn't ask for help with. Start by saying, "Can you help me?" Then, when they are done, make sure you let them know you appreciate their assistance by saying, "thank you."

Keep Up the Good Work

As you move through your week, make time to practice the concepts in this chapter. Remember to put one idea from your Action List into play to start improving your life, observe your tone of voice, and be willing to ask for help. If you think someone might have been rude to you, remember to ask for clarification. If you're feeling challenged, the following exercise can help you stay on track.

EXERCISE 6: Decide How You Will Stay Motivated

The following activities can help you maintain your commitment to reaching your relationship goals by keeping you motivated along the way. Choose any (or all) of the following suggestions:

- Read the statements on your 3 x 5 card (answers to the questions in Exercise 3) at the beginning of each day or as often as you need to personally stay committed to continuing the process.

- Read the Credo (found on page 180). If you like, download a free copy from our website to post somewhere you'll see regularly. Review it daily or as often as you like to remind you of the commitment you are making to yourself and your relationships.

If you are in a *More Love, More Joy!* Circle, the group will read the Credo together at the beginning of each meeting.

- Start a Love Poster. Create a collage of pictures, words, and statements that depict what your ideal love life looks like.

- Discover words that inspire you. If you find an affirmation or a few phrases that help you stay on track, write them down. Use sticky notes to help you remember. Place these reminders anywhere you'll see them on a regular basis.

- Keep in mind that by doing this work you can help others. When you show the world that you love yourself, you become a role model for your partner, children, co-workers, parents, and friends. Your words and actions set an example that may inspire those around you to see more possibilities inside themselves too.

- Stay connected with the *More Love, More Joy!* family. Visit the website or sign up for the mailing list to receive e-newsletters (e-news) and notices of events. Look for upcoming contests, events, and seminars. And, if you'd like, join a local peer-hosted Circle or start one of your own.

- Have fun. The more often you can laugh and play during this process the better. Take your time. Remember, learning can be graceful and easy if you let it.

Tip of the Week:
Honor your dreams and desires. You can have absolutely anything you want in your life. Take time this week to imagine the possibilities!

FOR CIRCLE MEMBERS

Week 2 Homework:
Complete prior to attending your 2nd Circle
- Read Chapter 3
- Do Exercises 2, 3, 4, & 5
- Complete your weekly commitment (from your Action List)

Bring to the Meeting:
- Your *More Love, More Joy!* book
- A journal/notebook and a pen/pencil

In Your Circle You Will Complete:
- Exercises 1 & 6
- Meditation

3

Opening the Door to More Love

"To love oneself is the beginning of a life-long romance."
~ Oscar Wilde

The foundation for a balanced and ever-evolving romantic relationship between two people begins with the love relationship each person has with themselves. In fact, the more we grow to love and accept ourselves, the greater our capacity becomes to allow another into our heart and into our lives. That's right; the more we love ourselves, the better we'll be able to experience love with someone else.

Learning to Love Myself

As far back as I can remember, I felt different. When I was a little girl I was shy and uncomfortable around people I didn't know. Looking back in time, I'm not certain if this was my true nature or just who I learned to be. My mother would introduce me by saying, "Jennifer is shy," as she assertively set out to help me make friends. I was curious about life, but at the time I felt unsure of myself. I knew then that "shy" wasn't normal and maybe not even good.

Sometime around the age of 4 or 5, I noticed I had a birthmark, a large, dark thumbprint on my light-skinned cheek. I felt vibrantly aware that I was marked and imperfect. By first grade, I knew the mark was a dividing line. I would never be considered as beautiful as all the other girls. Even when I would sometimes forget it was there, other people would be sure to point it out.

Fast forward to my pre-teen years. My body was on a course of its own. Regardless of what was "normal" or "average," my little 11-year-old frame had "developed." By the end of fifth grade, I had grown taller and curvier than the other girls. Perhaps I was even curvier than many of their mothers. I felt like Dolly Parton. I had been "blessed" with a tiny frame and enormous boobs. By my 12th birthday, I hated to go out of the house; being different felt excruciatingly painful.

I was ostracized by the other kids almost daily. If the name calling wasn't bad enough, the poking, pinching, and mean letters that arrived in my family's mailbox began to get to me. My own mother was clearly unprepared for my astonishing development. It was clear to me that this was something I would have to figure out on my own.

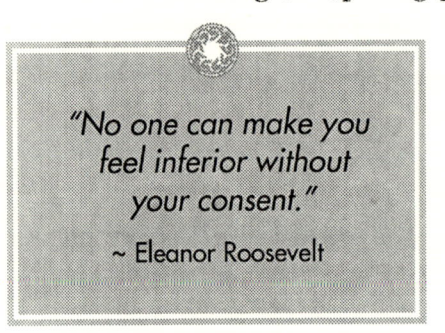

> "No one can make you feel inferior without your consent."
> ~ Eleanor Roosevelt

Just when I thought it couldn't get any worse, men of all ages started to notice me. I hated it. If this was what breasts were all about, I wished that I could have returned them. I did my best to be invisible, hiding my stained face and my gargantuan chest the best I could.

By the time I hit high school, I was pretty clear that I was doomed to be different. As much as I still wanted to fit in, it was easier to be a rebel. No matter what I faced, I pretended to have courage, which on some days felt almost impossible.

Somewhere I heard someone say, "Fake it 'til you make it," and this became my creed. I was determined not to let the rest of the world get the best of me, no matter how different I felt from everyone else.

As an adult, I finally realized that I didn't have to explain myself to anyone. I could tell politically incorrect jokes, dye my hair, or change my religion whenever it suited me. I was a free spirit. Whatever I felt inclined to do, I just did it, knowing that most people wouldn't understand.

Following my own path has not always been easy, but it has brought me great joy, a passion for living, and the pleasure of knowing that I am being true to myself. There is no doubt that I still have a lot to learn. Each day I continue to understand how to accept and love myself on a deeper level. In hindsight, I haven't always taken the easy path, but I can say with confidence that being courageous enough to sometimes only fit in with myself has paid off.

Now it's your turn; you can be as unique as you wish. Try something crazy, have the courage to be different. Give yourself permission to follow your heart instead of your head. And most of all, love yourself as you are. The following meditation will help you release other people's perceptions or judgements about who you are and help you to reclaim any aspects of your true self that you may have left behind.

Clean Slate Meditation: 14 minutes

Begin by closing your eyes. Take a deep breath in, and hold it. Exhaling very slowly, just relaxing and letting go of any tension, any tightness you might be holding in your body or your mind. And, another deep breath in, holding it as long as you comfortably can. And now, exhaling slowly and gently, becoming more and more relaxed with each breath. Just slowing down, and letting go. Breathing easily and gently, going deeper and deeper into a peaceful state of relaxation.

PAUSE 3 SECONDS . . .

And you know that you are perfectly safe here at this time. And no one and nothing can harm you. So you can just take your time to relax, let go, and unwind.

CONTINUED ▶

And you may begin to notice that your eyes are becoming comfortably closed. And your eyelids are starting to feel heavy. Heavy and so relaxed, calm and peaceful.

And a feeling of relaxation flows to your head and your face, as all the muscles in your head and face relax. Any tension or tightness is just beginning to melt away. You feel calm and peaceful, just like you do when you are about to drift off to sleep.

And now that gentle flow of relaxation moves into your shoulders and through your chest, as all the muscles of your shoulders and chest area relax. And that warm peaceful feeling flows down your arms and your back to the base of your spine, continuing down your legs all the way to the tips of your toes. Your mind is at ease and your entire body feels heavy, heavy and perfectly relaxed.

PAUSE 5 SECONDS...

Good. Now today you have been given the gift of transformation. No one and nothing can stop you from being everything you've always wanted to become. You can easily let go of any part of the past that might be holding you back and move gracefully into the most confident and evolved version of yourself imaginable. You are feeling good and feel excited about the possibilities before you.

Now imagine that you see a blackboard in front of you. And on that blackboard you write all the words that your inner critic or anyone else has ever used to describe you in a way that was unkind or unsupportive. Any words that negatively judged you, any labels that didn't represent who you really are deep down inside. Maybe you heard lazy, stupid, good for nothing, weak, or wishy washy. Not smart enough, not as good as the rest, too fat, or too selfish. Whatever you might have heard in the past that wasn't the truth, just see these words appear on the blackboard.

CONTINUED ▶

PAUSE FOR 10 SECONDS...

And you know deep down inside that these are only words and they are not the truth. They do not represent who you really are or your true potential. And today you are going to release them forever. From this point forward you are no longer going to be held back in any way by these labels or misperceptions.

Now I want you to think about your inner critic and all the people that may have said those untruths to you. And as you bring them to mind, one by one you can release both them and yourself from the past. Speaking with them now will free you from any judgments that were made.

So take a moment now to tell these people and any critical part of yourself, that what they said was NOT the truth. Those words did not represent who you really are and now you are letting go of all the hurt, all the pain, all the sadness, and any other unwanted emotions that these words or labels may have caused you to feel.

PAUSE 20 SECONDS...

Good. When you are done, thank them for coming today and say goodbye. Let them know that you will be interacting with them differently in the future, because you are no longer held back by their words, labels, or judgments.

So go back to that blackboard and erase all the words that you see. Just wipe them away, erasing them completely from who you are now. Those words are not a part of you any more. Those words do not describe who you really are. They are no longer yours. Those were only words and they are not you.

PAUSE 3 SECONDS...

Good. Now as you look at the blackboard, you see that it is beginning to display all the words that tell the truth—the words

CONTINUED ▶

that accurately describe the best version of you. You are happy, courageous, loving, intelligent, capable, self-confident, talented, valuable, interesting, and perfect, exactly as you are. And as you remember any other words that feel right for you, they will appear on the blackboard, and as they do, you can feel them taking hold within your body, your mind, and your spirit. So just feel how good it feels to allow the authentic you to be reborn and honored.

PAUSE 20 SECONDS...

Now take just another moment to feel thankful for remembering who you really are, and for the gift of releasing the past. From this point forward you can live your life authentically, with confidence, and a greater sense of peacefulness than you've ever experienced before.

PAUSE 5 SECONDS...

And now as I count from three to one you will become more awake, more alert, and ready to live your life fully. Confident and filled with love.

3 ... feeling full of natural vibrant energy,
2 ... filled with joy and happiness, and
1 ... eyes wide open, feeling good and ready to enjoy the rest of your day.

> ### Post Meditation
> Take a moment to consider what came to mind during your meditation and write down anything that will help remind you of who you really are.
>
> ### Circle Discussion:
> Take a few minutes after the meditation to exchange ideas about how each of you can stay true to the most empowered version of yourselves.

There's No Holding You Back

The words or labels that someone else might have given you no longer weigh you down. It's a new day and an opportunity for you and only you to decide who you really are from this point forward.

The next exercise will give you a chance to reacquaint yourself with all that you are and all that you intend to be. Have fun. Try to allow your potential to be limitless. Remember, you are perfect right here and right now.

EXERCISE 1: I am, I have, I know how to . . .

1. Start by taking a look at the list below. See how many of the words would describe you now or as you would like to be. Circle or check the words that describe the real you.

I am...

Accountable	Dynamic	Independent	Productive
Alert	Easy-Going	Innovative	Punctual
Appropriate	Effective	Inquisitive	Refined
Artistic	Empathetic	Intelligent	Reliable
Assertive	Empowered	Intentional	Resourceful
Astute	Energetic	Interesting	Respectful
Authentic	Engaging	Intuitive	Responsible
Aware	Enthusiastic	Joyful	Satisfied
Beautiful	Ethical	Kind	Self-Confident
Calm	Exceptional	Knowledgeable	Self-Reliant
Candid	Exciting	Likeable	Sensitive
Capable	Expressive	Loving	Sensual
Certain	Faithful	Loyal	Sincere
Committed	Firm	Magical	Smart
Communicative	Fit	Open-Minded	Spiritual
Compassionate	Flexible	Optimistic	Spontaneous
Confident	Free	Orderly	Stable
Conscientious	Friendly	Organized	Strong
Consistent	Generous	Patient	Stylish
Content	Gentle	Peaceful	Supportive
Cooperative	Handsome	Perfect	Tactful
Courageous	Happy	Playful	Talented
Creative	Healthy	Poised	Tidy
Curious	Honest	Polite	Trainable
Daring	Honorable	Positive	Trusting
Delightful	Humorous	Powerful	Truthful
Diplomatic	Imaginative	Practical	Versatile
Disciplined	Impressive	Proactive	Willing

2. Now complete the following questions with a few positive answers of your own.

   "I" sentences

   Examples: I adapt well. I ask for what I need. I initiate things.
   I present myself well. I manage my time well.

   I _____.

   I _____.

   "I am a" sentences

   Examples: I am a contributor. I am a leader. I am a planner. I am a problem-solver. I am a good listener.

   I am a _____.

   I am a _____.

   I am a _____.

   "I have" sentences

   Examples: I have clear boundaries. I have a sense of humor.
   I have a willingness to try new things.

   I have _____.

   I have _____.

   I have _____.

   "I know how to" sentences

   Examples: I know how to be intimate with someone I love.
   I know how to have fun. I know how to sing well.

   I know how to _____.

   I know how to _____.

EXERCISE 2: Tooting Your Own Horn

I had a mentor who used to say, "If you don't toot your own horn, you can't hear the music." Since we sometimes forget to honor our personal accomplishments, practice "tooting your own horn" a bit. Each of us has done something we didn't know we could accomplish or has overcome something we once considered an obstacle.

Choose two or three of the scenarios below. Write in your journal whatever you recall. This is a great way to remind yourself of how amazing you actually are, that you have the capacity for greatness, and that you *can* do things you might have thought were too difficult or impossible.

> "Let your light shine. Shine within you so that it can shine on someone else. Let your light shine."
>
> ~ Oprah Winfrey

- Think back to a time when you may have earned an award or were honored for doing something well. Write down what you can remember about that experience.

- Do you remember any challenges you might have overcome? What about learning how to swim, learning a new skill for work, or quitting smoking? What was the driving force that helped you to achieve your goal?

- Think of a situation when you allowed yourself to shine, or when you tried something for the first time (maybe your first kiss, tasting a new food, or riding in an airplane). Do you remember how you felt before? And after?

- Think of an instance when you were courageous. Did you ever stand up for something you believed in? Did you do something that felt impossible but you knew you had to do it anyway? Where did you find the strength to get it done?

- Was there a time in your life when you overcame adversity? How did you go about making changes in your life? What did you learn about yourself from this experience?

- Did you ever get hurt or were you ill and then you healed? How did you feel about life when you came through it all? Did you learn something about yourself through the process?

Choosing to be Happy

As you complete these exercises, I hope that you are being reminded of how incredible you are and what you have accomplished in your life. You can do anything, including changing your attitudes and feelings. The great truth of the matter is that only *you* can "make *you* happy." No one else has that power, unless you give them complete control over your feelings, thoughts, and your freedom of choice. Happy is something *you* choose to be when and if *you* like.

You've probably heard the analogy that some people perceive situations as a glass half-full while others see the glass as half-empty. This illustrates the point that two people can be looking at the very same circumstance and both have different outlooks on what is actually taking place. Some see things positively (glass half-full) and others see things in the opposite way (glass half-empty). Neither view is right nor wrong; each is only one person's perception of reality.

The choice of how you perceive the glass (or anything else in your life) is yours. The way you respond to what you see and experience is also up to you. Your thoughts and feelings are really decisions you make whether they are made consciously or unconsciously. These choices are what create your reality. Therefore, your happiness is not dependent upon anyone or anything else, you just need to make that choice.

We encourage you to take the time to discover what "makes you happy." In this book, we have used this statement because people understand its meaning (even if the actual words feel in conflict to our beliefs). We hope that you are willing to look beyond the words that we've used and identify what you personally enjoy rather than what "makes you" happy (or anything else). Take responsibility for your choice to be happy instead of giving your power away to someone else.

COMMUNICATION TIPS

🗨️ Using "I Feel" Messages

If you want your partner (or anyone you communicate with) to actually hear what you are saying, the way you phrase your sentences is important. By using "I feel" messages, you take responsibility for the way you feel (which is more productive than placing blame on your partner).

The Formula:

> "When you _____(fill in the blank)_____,
> I feel_____(fill in the blank)_____."

This technique often keeps the listener from being triggered into a defensive mode which can divert their focus, making it difficult for them to reply in the way you wish. See if you can imagine how someone might respond to the following sample statements.

Rather than saying:

> "You are always late for dinner. I can't believe if you loved me you would treat me this way."

Change it to:

> "When you are late for our dinner dates, I feel disrespected."

Improve an "I Feel" Message by Requesting Action

Being able to communicate how you feel is important, but this alone will not typically help you get more of what you want in your life. However, when you combine an "I feel" message with a statement giving your partner the benefit of the doubt and a specific request for action, you will realize the true power of this technique. Here's how it works:

> **Step 1:** Start with a statement giving your partner the benefit of the doubt. Say something positive that will get them listening. For example: "Honey, I know that you love me and want me to feel cared for in our relationship."

Step 2: Use your "I feel" message. For example: "So I want to let you know that when you are late to our dinner dates, I feel disrespected."

Step 3: Follow with a kind request for what you would like in the future. For example: "Do you think that next time we make plans, you can be here on time?"

Now you try. Practice identifying your true feelings and using "I feel" messages to request specific actions this week.

⌨ Show a Little Self-Respect

The way you communicate with yourself aloud becomes an indicator for how it would be acceptable for others to treat you. Your internal conversations or self-talk works the same way. If you make a mistake and the first thing that you think (or that comes out of your mouth) is, "Nice going, idiot," then you have announced to yourself and the world that you are in fact an idiot (and should be treated as such). Do your best to treat yourself with love and kindness and others will be more likely to do the same.

EXERCISE 3: Self-Talk and Self-Respect

What messages are you sending to yourself and others through your self-talk and self-directed actions?

1. Observe the way you use self-talk (the voice you hear in your head or when you talk to yourself out loud). Are your words kind and loving, or are they rude, abusive, or mean? Is this the most respectful way that you would speak to someone you care for? If you do have an inner critic who isn't very supportive, fire 'em! There's no reason to hang out with anyone who isn't very nice.

2. Watch your actions when you make reference to yourself in front of others. When you mess up, do you hit yourself in the head and say, "What was I thinking?" You wouldn't like it if someone else hit you in the head, so why do it yourself? Fire this one, too.

3. Be mindful of how you show others you like to be treated. Keep some notes to help you remember anything you'd like to improve. Remember to try to use the most kind, loving, and supportive words. Imagine you love yourself, or treat yourself the way you wish someone else would.

4. Try not to "should" on yourself. Replace your "shoulds" with "coulds" and remember that everything you do is your choice.

EXERCISE 4: Discover Your Own Supportive Affirmations

Affirmations give power and energy to the process of creation. Every time you speak, write, read, or imagine what it feels like to have what you are affirming, you participate in bringing it into your life.

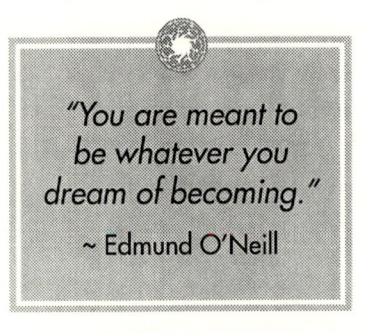

> *"You are meant to be whatever you dream of becoming."*
> ~ Edmund O'Neill

You can use sticky notes to post an affirmation anywhere. Put them on the dashboard of your car, your bathroom mirror, or anywhere else you might look on a daily basis to help you remember your commitments. If you are feeling creative, buy some special Crayola® markers that will enable you to temporarily write your affirmations on bathroom mirrors. Feel free to use affirmations in whatever way feels right for you.

Are there any words you could use to help you remember you are wonderful and worthy of being loved? Write down a few ideas of your own or use one of the following suggestions, then review them daily.

- When I speak kindly to myself, I know I am in alignment with the Divine.

- My opinion is valid and worthy of sharing.

- I am lovable just as I am and I am worthy of being a part of a balanced and mutually supportive love relationship.

- When I treat myself kindly and with love, I am a living example of how others should treat me.

EXERCISE 5: What is Your "Something Wonderful?"

When was the last time you did something special just for you? Your assignment every week from this point forward is to find at least 15-minutes to take yourself out on a date or do something wonderful for yourself. If you don't do this regularly, then it's a great time to get into the habit. How can you treat yourself special this week?

1. **15-minute Pick Me Up**

    What could you do for yourself in a 15-minute time frame that would bring you joy? Here are a few ideas:

    - Call a friend who tells stories that always result in laughter.

    - Cruise the Internet for ideas for your next vacation, an upcoming sporting event, or a concert you'd like to attend.

    - Read a magazine or newspaper column you enjoy.

2. **One Hour Getaway**

    What could you do for yourself in an hour? How about:

    - Getting a manicure or massage.

    - Heading to the driving range to hit a bucket of balls.

    - Taking yourself for a walk in the park.

3. **Day (or an Evening) to Yourself**

    Go ahead, be decadent. Stop waiting for someone else to "make" you feel happy. Give yourself a day of something wonderful!

    - Go shopping for something you wouldn't normally buy (even if you don't purchase it). Maybe you would enjoy test driving that new Jaguar or Porsche?

    - Try a restaurant you've been meaning to visit. Take a book and then you'll get reading time along with a great meal!

    - Spend a day in the spa getting pampered.

    - Visit a museum that you haven't been to in awhile.

EXERCISE 6: Contract to Care for Yourself with Love

When was the last time you made your personal needs and happiness a priority? Consider making a commitment to take care of yourself in the most loving way imaginable. What could you do differently or more regularly that would help you feel more balanced or fulfilled? How could you treat yourself with more respect, love, and kindness?

Think about making a contract that will motivate you personally to care for your body, mind, and spirit. Use the categories below to remind you of different aspects of your life that you might want to include in your contract. Record your thoughts or use any artistic expression you desire.

So go ahead, make your own contract to love and care for yourself. You can renew it as long as you like or revise it when it doesn't reflect what works for you anymore. Write it down, read it out loud, and then sign it. This is a great step toward honoring your personal needs and creating more joy, fulfillment, peace, ease, confidence, or whatever else you wish for in your life.

You will find two sample contracts on the following pages. Use them to inspire your own personal version.

> *"You, yourself, as much as anybody in the entire universe, deserve your love and affection."*
>
> ~ Buddha

Some Categories to Consider:

- ☐ Attitude/Outlook
- ☐ Body Image
- ☐ Commitments
- ☐ Communication
- ☐ Family (Extended)
- ☐ Family (Immediate)
- ☐ Finances
- ☐ Friends
- ☐ Health/Exercise
- ☐ Hobbies
- ☐ Home Life
- ☐ Love Life
- ☐ Personal Time
- ☐ Self Care
- ☐ Self Talk
- ☐ Spirituality/Religion
- ☐ Travel
- ☐ Work

Sample Contract 1

- I am committed to positive self-talk. I will remember that everything I think, feel, and say can eventually become my reality.

- I will do my best to remember that loving my body as it is will help me look and feel youthful, alive, happy, and healthy.

- I will remember that sometimes the journey is more important than getting to the destination. Not everything in life needs to happen quickly.

- I am committed to speaking my truth and asking for what I want from everyone and, most importantly, from myself.

- I am committed to being kind and loving to myself and to forgiving myself as often as I need to.

- I will listen to my body. I will give it rest when it needs it, water when it is thirsty, and food when it is hungry.

- I will remember that I am a part of the world and will take responsibility for my actions. My intention is to do my best to respect the earth and world around me.

- I am committed to loving my partner with honesty and integrity. I am willing to ask for what I really want.

- I will live my life today and everyday courageously, always remembering that everything happens for a reason. I will trust my heart and know I am always on the right path.

- I am committed to more being and less doing. And, I am committed to saying my affirmations and energy dedications every morning and evening.

_____   _____
Signed   Date

Sample Contract 2

- I pledge to experience and acknowledge the wholeness of my being as my Divine gift.

- I intend to accept and love myself as I am and as I become, without apology or explanation.

- I promise to follow my heart and speak my truth even when I believe that others will not understand.

- I promise to be gentle with myself as I learn and grow through my experiences.

- I claim full responsibility for myself and my actions.

- I commit to living in the "coulds" rather than the "shoulds," with the knowledge that my actions and choices are always an exercise of my own free-will.

- I claim my Divine right to co-create experiences that bring me joy, happiness, love, abundance, wellness, and wholeness.

- I commit to living in partnership with my body, to water it, feed it, and tend to it as I would a valued friend.

- I promise to develop and grow relationships in accordance with universal balance and harmony, based on the principle of equal exchange.

- I commit to gracefully releasing anything that is not in my highest and best good.

- I gratefully accept the gifts and opportunities the universe presents.

_____   _____
Signed   Date

Make Your Weekly Commitment
Choose one step you'll take this week from your Action List (from Chapter 2) to make progress toward your relationship goals.

Keep Up the Good Work
Complete your contract and read it every morning to start your day off with a positive reminder of the commitment you are making to love and care for yourself. Remember, no matter what circumstances you find yourself in this week, you can choose to see the "glass half-full." Be grateful for the good in your life. Practice requesting action using your "I feel" messages and fire your inner critic if you notice your self-talk isn't very supportive. Treat yourself this week to your something wonderful and celebrate the positive changes you are experiencing in your life.

> **Tip of the Week:**
> Happiness is your choice. What can you do this week to experience more happiness in your life?

FOR CIRCLE MEMBERS

Week 3 Homework:
Complete prior to attending your 3rd Circle
- Read Chapter 4
- Do Exercises 1, 2, & 7
- Complete your weekly commitment

Bring to the Meeting:
- Your *More Love, More Joy!* book
- A journal/notebook and a pen/pencil
- Your completed Exercises 1 and 2
- 1-2 affirmations (from Exercise 7)
- Art supplies for Exercise 4 (see pg. 73 for full list): poster board, markers, pens, magazines, etc.

In Your Circle You Will Complete:
- Exercises 3-6
- Meditation

4

What Have You Learned About Love?

"As soon as you trust yourself, you will know how to live."
~ Johann Wolfgang von Goethe

There once was a young girl, the oldest of three, whose parents got a divorce when she was 13-years-old. Prior to the divorce, she can only remember screaming; raised voices in the bedroom and lots of anger and tears.

She can't really recall a time when her parents held hands or kissed. They always seemed too busy to hold her on their laps (she was a big girl now). It wasn't a priority to tell her that they loved her or how proud they were of her. She was no longer a baby and was old enough to be the helper (whether she liked it or not).

At 19, she found herself in her first romantic relationship with someone who had picked her. He loved her through sex. He even told her she was beautiful during sex. He was charming and handsome, although not especially available. But the girl felt satisfied knowing that at least someone loved her now.

She didn't have his telephone number. He came around often enough didn't he? At least twice a week when she finished working her early shifts as a cocktail waitress, he walked her home, had sex with her, and then left. Occasionally she'd see him during the day for a few hours before he went to work (as a Hawaiian dancer in a tourist show). When they were together she was in love, and when he wasn't there, she waited. Waited . . . and cried.

Fast forward to our little one's mid-20s. She knew by now that she could pick the men she dated and she didn't have to wait for whoever came along to find her attractive. She knew that she held the cards when it came to sex. She realized she could sleep with pretty much with anyone she wanted. If she felt like being held, told how beautiful she was, or even occasionally hear the words, "I love you," she knew that through sex she could get what she wanted. She discovered how she could feel loved on her own schedule.

She had new rules and boundaries now. No married men, no body builders on steroids, no one who was abusive, no one with a smaller butt than hers, no one who wanted a brainless set of tits and ass, and no one that was just looking for a baby-making machine to complete his life. She only wanted true love.

> *"Love yourself first and everything else falls into line."*
> ~ Lucille Ball

At 28 the girl found herself in a relationship again. He was charming, funny, interesting, and aloof. An artist. He had so many talents that he didn't even recognize. (Good thing that she did.) Of course, he found her equally amazing: clever, intelligent, moving quickly up the corporate ladder, a homeowner, pet lover, a great cook, and with a hot bod (most of the time when she wasn't yo-yo dieting).

They held hands, gave each other massages, kissed a lot, and had a secret language all their own. Together they enjoyed so many of the same things.

She loved him. They told each other they loved one another. And, if he didn't flirt with girls at parties and have a few female friendships that were exclusive of her, she probably would have believed him.

All in all, it was the best times so far for her. But after a year or so, she found herself crying. A lot. She still believed that their relationship was still good, wasn't it? She was only crying 25% of the time.

Twenty-five percent of the time! That meant that if they got together four or five nights out of the week, she would spend one entire evening wracked with tears. Could this really be the man that she wanted to spend the rest of her life with?

For the longest time she thought that this might be all right. When it was good, it was great and after all, she was only crying 25% of the time. It could have been 50%, right?

Eventually our girl had an epiphany. She finally decided to move on from this romance with "Mr. Right" with whom she only found herself crying 25% of the time.

The 25% rule was huge. Where could she possibly have learned that crying during one-fourth of her relationship might have been acceptable? Was this something she learned from her parents? Regardless, she vowed never to repeat this pattern again.

> "Only I can change my life. No one can do it for me."
> ~ Carol Burnett

Hopefully, we all walk away from our relationships feeling as though we learned something. At each new beginning we can choose to have new rules or boundaries. There are things that we will never do again (like cry 25% of the time, or be in relationships with people who are separated, but still legally married, not like I'd ever know anything about that).

We all have our stories of love, but where did we learn what was "normal," what was okay, or what we might aspire to create in our own lives? Are you limiting yourself by living out someone else's rules and beliefs about love? If there are habits or patterns in your love life that you're ready to break, read on to discover more.

EXERCISE 1: What Did You Learn About Romantic Love?

Begin by writing "Romantic Love" at the top of your journal or notebook. You will be making a list and recording what you were taught (either intentionally or unintentionally) about romantic love by your "love role models." This can include what they told you was right for you or how they modeled love through their actions. As you look back, note if there were different rules for people you dated versus people you married.

The intention here is to identify both healthy habits and beliefs as well as any undesirable patterns you've learned. In this chapter, you'll have an opportunity to rediscover and reclaim anything you would like to honor and enjoy more of in your own life. You'll also have the chance to release any behaviors you recognize yourself repeating that no longer feel like a good fit.

If you find that while you are answering the following questions that you can't remember the specifics, see if any impressions or feelings that come to mind. Now, review the questions below to spark your memories, and then write down whatever you recall.

What did your parents or other role models teach you about romantic love?

1. What did love romantic love look like? Was it an arranged marriage? Were both people young, or old? Was it something you could see?

2. What words did they say to each other to express their love for each other? Were they kind? Respectful? Did they use pet names?

3. What tones of voice do those in romantic love use? Did they speak in whispers? Could they yell at each other and still be in love?

4. How did they express their love to each other or someone they cared for? Did they send flowers? Hold hands? Write love letters?

5. When was it appropriate to show romantic love and when wasn't it? Where was it okay to show your love and where was it off limits?

6. Who did you learn was appropriate for you or your role models to love romantically? Was any race, religion, age, or gender not considered to be acceptable?

7. How do people who love each other romantically touch each other? Are there different rules for in public vs. in private?

8. What did they do when things got tough? Yell? Throw things? Say they want a divorce? Communicate? See a counselor? Shut down or run away? Do bad things and then make it up with good things? If things didn't work out, was divorce an option or did they stay together no matter what?

9. What other rules were there (either spoken or unspoken)?

Now Rate What You've Listed

As you review your notes, rate the answers you wrote on a 1-10 scale. Ten would be something you would consider the best-case scenario, something you believe in completely, and 1 would be something you don't relate to or agree with at all.

In looking through your notes, did you find rules, habits, or patterns from your role models that you recognize in your own life? Have your actions in current (or past) relationships reflected your own values or those of your role models? Take time to record anything that comes to mind.

> *"Trust your heart, it will always know the path to your truth."*
>
> ~ Jennifer Martin

Note: Keep your rated lists for this exercise (Exercise 1) and Exercise 2 on hand. They will be used later in the chapter for the meditation and then an art project (Exercise 4).

EXERCISE 2: What Did You Learn About Self-Love?

This exercise will repeat similar steps to those covered in Exercise 1. This time, begin by writing "Self-Love" at the top of your journal or notebook. Now, consider what your parents or other role models taught you about caring for yourself. How did they model self-love and care? How did they teach you to love yourself? Where did they place themselves on their own priority list? The idea here is to record whatever you can remember, recognizing both what you felt was valuable and anything you don't want to (or no longer want to) repeat.

1. What did loving and taking care of oneself look like? Did your role models take good care of their own needs? Did they respect their own boundaries? Did they live their lives in balance? Did they do nice things for themselves?

2. What words did they use when talking about themselves? Were they confident and strong, self-pitying, apologetic, or humble?

3. What priority did your role models give to caring for themselves? Did they put other people's needs before themselves? Or did they primarily take care of number one?

4. If they felt proud, was it appropriate to let people know what they had accomplished? Could they take credit for a job well done? How did your role models handle this in their lives?

5. How was self-respect and self-worth displayed? Were the rules different for men versus women? Did you learn that your self-worth was related to the color of your skin, your educational level, your financial status, your age, your nationality, religion, or any other characteristics you can remember?

6. If you recall your role models making "mistakes," how easy (or challenging) was it for them to forgive themselves?

7. Was there anything they taught you that was necessary to say, be, or do in order to be worthy of being loved by someone else?

8. What other rules were there, either spoken or unspoken, about how you should care for or love yourself?

Now Rate What You've Listed
Follow the same format as Exercise 1. Rate your answers on a 1-10 scale and save your notes for later.

Optional: If you'd like to delve a little deeper into these topics, we encourage you to journal about what you've discovered or answer the questions from the following Circle discussion in Exercise 3.

> ### CIRCLE EXERCISE 3: Discussion
>
> Take a few minutes to share some of the things you were taught that surprised you. What did you learn about your beliefs or habits? Below are some questions to consider.
>
> 1. How have you noticed that your ideals are different from the generation(s) before yours or those of your role models?
> 2. What patterns do you see yourself repeating even though they may not feel right for you?
> 3. Did you recall any positive behaviors, beliefs, or habits that your love role models displayed that you would like to incorporate into your own life?

Release the Rules You No Longer Want

Now that you have discovered a little more about how you learned what was right for you in love, you may better understand why it is that you do the things you do. Regardless of how your love role models may have influenced you, now it is your job to follow your heart and love yourself and others in your own way.

If you discovered that you are repeating some of what you learned and it no longer feels right for you, then give these "love rules" back and begin to embrace a new way of doing things that is just right for you. Be willing to keep trying something new until your actions feel in harmony with your heart and your mind.

In the following meditation, you will have a chance to honor your love role models for anything you learned about love that felt of value to you. During this time, you can also return to them any of their love rules that no longer feel like your own. Are you ready? Relax, enjoy, and let go!

Releasing Others' Rules About Love
Meditation: 14 minutes

Begin by closing your eyes. Take a deep breath in, and hold it. Exhaling very slowly, just relaxing and letting go of any tension, any tightness you might be holding in your body or your mind. And, another deep breath in, holding it as long as you comfortably can. And now, exhaling slowly and gently, becoming more and more relaxed with each breath. Just slowing down, and letting go. Breathing easily and gently, going deeper and deeper into a peaceful state of relaxation.

PAUSE 3 SECONDS . . .

And you know that you are perfectly safe here at this time. And no one and nothing can harm you. So you can just take your time to relax, let go, and unwind.

And you may begin to notice that your eyes are becoming comfortably closed. And your eyelids are starting to feel heavy. Heavy and so relaxed, calm and peaceful.

And a feeling of relaxation flows to your head and your face, as all the muscles in your head and face relax. Any tension or tightness is just beginning to melt away. You feel calm and peaceful, just like you do when you are about to drift off to sleep.

And now that gentle flow of relaxation moves into your shoulders and through your chest, as all the muscles of your shoulders and chest area relax. And that warm peaceful feeling flows down your arms and your back to the base of your spine, continuing down your legs all the way to the tips of your toes. Your mind is at ease and your entire body feels heavy, heavy and perfectly relaxed.

CONTINUED ▶

PAUSE 5 SECONDS...

Now imagine you are in the most incredible place you can think of. Maybe a beautiful sandy beach or somewhere out in nature. Any place that comes to mind is fine, just so long as you feel peaceful and comfortable. Good. So take a moment to get a feel for this perfect place. And as you begin to look around, you notice that you are surrounded by angels.

The angels have joined you today to help you release and transform any love rules you may have been taught about loving yourself or loving others that are no longer of use to you. They will help you begin to gracefully start loving yourself and others in harmony with what truly feels right for you.

The angels want you to know that you are never alone, and that they love you, unconditionally. You are perfect just as you are. So take a moment to experience what it feels like to be divinely loved. To be honored, accepted, and respected, just for being you. Experience what this divine love feels like on your skin, in your heart, tingling throughout your entire body.

PAUSE 10 SECONDS...

Good. Now your angels ask you to bring to mind your love role models, the people who may have taught you what it looks like to be loved, or to be in love, and how you were supposed to love yourself and those you care about. Now ask your love role models if they would join you here, in this perfect place with your angels. Regardless of what your history might have been together, you notice that as they arrive you feel perfectly at ease. You can feel the pure essence of love from your angels and you notice that everyone appears peaceful and comfortable.

You know in your heart that it will be safe to speak honestly. So tell your love role models that you realize now that some of

CONTINUED ▶

what they taught you about the way to love yourself and love others isn't right for you anymore. These rules aren't the best way or the only way for you to love anymore. Today, you are returning any rules back to them that were theirs and no longer serve you.

And let them know that from this point forward you will be following your heart. That you will trust yourself to determine what is right for you when it comes to loving others and caring for yourself. You can now share with them anything you want to about your experiences together, knowing in your heart that speaking the words of truth will set you free.

PAUSE 10 SECONDS...

Now thank them and let them know how much you learned because of them or in spite of them, and be sure to credit them for any positive things they taught you about love.

PAUSE 10 SECONDS...

Goood. Feel how free and liberated you are after sharing your true feelings. How much lighter you feel. You are more at ease, more relaxed, and completely peaceful. And from this point forward, you can gently begin a new phase in your life through the way you love others and how you love and care for yourself.

So thank your angels and your love role models for coming today and for loving you and supporting you as you learn how to love and honor yourself. And when you are ready, say goodbye for now.

PAUSE 3 SECONDS...

Now that you are free of the past, take a moment to imagine yourself in the near future. See yourself treating those you care for with love in the way that feels right for you. Notice how you

CONTINUED ▶

are treating yourself with more love, kindness, and compassion. What do you notice has changed? How do you feel? Are you more peaceful? More free? More vibrant or alive? Just take a moment to experience what this new way of loving feels like and notice how grateful you are for this positive change in your life.

PAUSE 15 SECONDS...

Good. Now take just another moment to feel thankful for remembering who you really are and for the gift of releasing the past. From this point forward you can live authentically with greater confidence and more peacefulness.

PAUSE 5 SECONDS...

And now as I count from three to one you will become more awake, more alert, and ready to live your life fully. Confident and filled with love.

3... feeling full of natural vibrant energy,
2... filled with joy and happiness, and
1... eyes wide open, feeling good and ready to enjoy the rest of your day.

EXERCISE 4: Create Your New "Love Rules"

What you'll need: Oversized paper or poster board, pens, markers, photos, magazines for clippings, stickers, glitter, glue, or whatever else will help you make your "love rules" poster memorable and meaningful. (Consider these to be love guidelines, not really rules.)

1. **Review Your Notes from Exercises 1 & 2**

   Take another look at your notes about how your role models taught you to love and care for yourself and your partner. Review the "rules" that you rated a 7 or higher. These are the concepts you consider to be healthy, balanced, and worth repeating.

2. **Consider Your Personal Experience**
   Is there anything else you've learned or discovered about love that you would like to become part of your new love guidelines?

3. **Create Your Own Love Rules or Guiding Principles**
   You can write your ideas down, make a collage, draw pictures, or create your love rules poster in whatever way you wish. There is no judgment here, as this is just an opportunity to honor what you learned and to cultivate more of what you want in your own life. Focus on the positive and what you want for your future.

COMMUNICATION TIPS

[TIP] The Power of Acknowledging

When you communicate with others in a kind and respectful way, your chances of having successful conversations improve dramatically. One way you can communicate with kindness is to acknowledge the person you are in conversation with.

For clarification, acknowledging is not agreeing. It is a polite and considerate way to recognize the person speaking by letting them know that you are listening. It also communicates that you understand that what they are talking about is important to them (regardless of whether or not it is to you).

Start by making eye contact, and try to allow the other person to speak freely, without cutting them off. Let them know you are listening by saying, "Okay," or by reflecting back what you hear, such as, "I can tell that you are really upset." Do your best to respect their thoughts and give the person your full attention.

If someone is making a point or is asking you to do something, it is always good to make sure you heard them correctly. Acknowledge them by saying, "So what you're telling me is . . . ", or "What I thought you just said was . . ." and repeat in your own words what they told you. This is a direct approach to clarifying up front what is being said and is a respectful way of letting the other person know that you are indeed listening.

🔖 Honoring Your Boundaries & Saying "No"

Can you remember a time when someone asked you for help with something, and without even thinking you said, "yes"? Or, has your partner ever requested you make a compromise that was uncomfortable for you, but you agreed to it anyway?

Learning how to say, "no," can be a challenge for anyone. Keep in mind that remembering to honor your own boundaries and priorities is one of the most loving ways to take care of yourself.

If you've ever felt guilty about saying, "no," this feeling might indicate that you are experiencing inner conflict. Inside, you may not want to agree, but another aspect of yourself may feel that you "should." If this happens, change your perspective. Replace the "should" with a "could." If you remember you have a choice about the matter, it can be easier to see your options more clearly. Then, if you want to be kind and loving to someone, rather than just doing what they ask (if that doesn't feel quite right for you), consider another way you can tell or show them you care.

> *"Saying no can be the ultimate self-care."*
> ~ Claudia Black

So, the next time someone in your personal life requests that you take on a responsibility, do something, or make a compromise, stop and listen to your heart. In your mind, focus your attention inward and consider if meeting this request feels true to you. Maintaining your inner peace and sense of balance isn't selfish, it's essential. Listen to the little voice inside and respond accordingly. Don't be afraid to say, "no."

🔖 How to Say "No"

So if you want to say, "no," or respectfully disagree with someone, how do you do it? It's easy when you combine these three elements together into one sentence:

Step 1: Begin the Sentence by Acknowledging
Let the other person know that you are listening and you recognize their request is important to them.

Step 2: Then Add the Conjunction "And"
Connect both thoughts using the word "and."

Step 3: Finish by Respectfully Stating Your Position
Confidently state your decision or thoughts. Be honest and try not to give excuses.

Keep in mind, not everyone may hear you the first time around. You may need to repeat this pattern a few times. Stick with it and the other person will eventually see that you are not going back down.

Example:

John: "I'm having such a difficult time finding helpers for the park clean-up event this year. Can I count on you to help recruit people?"

Stephanie: "I know that this is a really big project and you could use my help, *and* unfortunately, I just can't commit to any additional work right now."

🔖 Keep Your "But" to Yourself
Resist the temptation to use a "but" in place of your "and." Sometimes when people hear a "but" they feel it discounts or negates everything that came before it. When you keep your "but" to yourself, you can remain true to your own interests or position without disrespecting or disregarding the other person's concerns.

EXERCISE 5: Just Say "No"
Either on your own or with a partner, respond to the following requests. Practice saying, "no," using the conjunction "and."

1. **Your partner asks:**

   "Would you mind talking to my mother to tell her that we can't make Thanksgiving this year?" The two of you have agreed to vacation over the holiday and you would prefer if your partner handled telling their parents. How do you respond?

2. **A neighbor asks:**

   "Could you watch my kids over the weekend?" You don't want her kids at your house all weekend. What do you tell her?

3. **Your boss asks:**

   "We need another player on the company softball team. Can we count on you?" The games are on the same evening you reserve for date nights and you don't want to give that up. What do you say?

🗨️ Diplomatically & Respectfully Disagreeing

The conjunction "and" is also effective when someone is telling you what to do. You *can* acknowledge the other person's opinion respectfully, while staying true to what feels right for you. Remember that sometimes people are attached to their opinions and may not be ready to let you to make your own decisions right away. Follow along as Sally acknowledges Colleen's opinion without conceding her decision.

Sample Dialogue:

Colleen: "Sally, I really think that you are making the wrong decision marrying Bob, especially since this is his fourth marriage. I don't want you to get hurt again."

Sally: "Colleen, I appreciate that you want to take care of me *and* I love Bob. I promise you I am going into this with my eyes open. We are going to get married."

Colleen: "Sweetie, I'm sorry, but this is really a mistake. You are moving to fast. Couldn't you just date a while longer? Maybe a year isn't enough time to get to know him."

Sally: "I know that you love me, *and* I'm committed to getting married to Bob. I appreciate your concerns and I don't really want to talk about anymore."

Colleen: "Okay, Sally, but I really think this is a bad move."

Sally: "Thanks, I appreciate your honesty."

EXERCISE 6: Disagreeing Using the Conjunction "And"

On your own or with a partner, practice respectfully responding to the following requests using the conjunction "and." Follow the format from the example with Colleen and Sally.

Scenarios:

1. You are considering a job offer doing something you've always wanted to do that pays less than your current job. Your best friend says, "You shouldn't be accepting a job making less money, especially since you've been complaining about not being able to pay off your credit cards." How do you reply?

2. Your sister's marriage is on the rocks because her husband is rarely home to help take care of the kids. You try to help her when you can, but your life is jam packed, too. She calls again to ask for help and your partner says, "You've got to stop jumping to help your sister every time she calls." What do you tell your partner?

3. You have a history with not sticking to an exercise plan. This time you feel like something has changed and you are more committed than ever. When you tell your brother you've hired a trainer, he says: "Why do you want to waste your money when you know you'll never keep up with it?" What do you say?

EXERCISE 7: Affirmations

On a piece of paper or a sticky note, write down an affirmation for the week. How can you remind yourself of the way you want to love? Make up your own or adopt one of the affirmations below:

- When I allow myself to love completely, life feels light and easy.
- When I love in a balanced way, my life is abundant and filled with joy.
- I am open and ready to be in a committed relationship with someone who is available and feels the same way.

EXERCISE 8: Bless & Release Your Love Role Models (optional)

Using whatever artistic expression you wish, bless and release your parents (or other role models) for teaching you about love. If you are feeling particularly appreciative, you can write your role models a thank you note (even if they have passed away) to let them know how you feel about what you learned from them.

Note:
Keep in mind that sometimes you can learn from what doesn't work for you. For example, if you grew up in a household where your parents were not especially nice to one another and as a result you've chosen a relationship with someone who *is* supportive, considerate, kind, and loving, then by default, what you learned was a blessing even though the circumstances may not have seemed ideal. Every experience, good or bad, can present an opportunity to create change in your life.

EXERCISE 9: Flush & Release (optional)

Is there an emotion, habit, pattern, or relationship that you are ready to let go of once and for all? Keep a pen by your toilet. When you want to release something that no longer serves you (i.e. "feeling I am not worthy of unconditional love"), just write the thought down on the toilet paper. Make the intention to release this thought from every aspect of your being and flush it away.

Make Your Weekly Commitments

Choose a step from your Action List (from Chapter 2) that you will complete this week to make progress toward your relationship goals. Also, spend some time doing "something wonderful" just for you.

> **Tip of the Week:**
> Be the love role model you may have wished you had! You are lovable, perfect, and deserving of receiving the love you want. Treat yourself like you are worth it!

FOR CIRCLE MEMBERS

Week 4 Homework:
Complete prior to attending your 4th Circle
- Read Chapter 5
- Do Exercises 3 & 5
- Complete your weekly commitments

Bring to the Meeting:
- Your *More Love, More Joy!* book
- A journal/notebook and a pen/pencil
- Thoughts about your experience doing Exercise 3

In Your Circle You Will Complete:
- Exercises 1, 2, & 4
- Meditation

5

Forgiveness & Letting Go of the Past

*"If you want others to be happy, practice compassion.
If you want to be happy, practice compassion."*
~ Dalai Lama

There is no question that I am my own worst critic. For 11 years I worked at the same company and for most of that time I had the same boss. I handled some extremely valuable assets and made the company millions of dollars each and every year. My career was something I took very seriously, doing whatever it took to get the job done. Fortunately, my hard work and dedication was appreciated and recognized by my supervisors. I was the best at what I did, earning the highest salary nationwide for a person in my position.

And then it happened. One day in my ninth year, I made a mistake. A big mistake. An $8,000 mistake. How could I explain this to my boss and his boss? I agonized over what was going to happen to me and decided that I could just let them take the $8,000 from my future paychecks. Obviously, I could no longer be trusted. I thought about quitting. Wouldn't that be better than being fired? It was then that I broke the cardinal rule for women, don't cry at work, and went into my boss's office sobbing to serve my letter of resignation.

Needless to say, if you were paying attention, I worked for this company for 11 years, and the "biggie" took place in my ninth year. When I proposed serving my resignation, my boss started laughing.

He couldn't believe I was serious after all I had done to meet deadlines, come in under budget and ahead of schedule, and achieve things that people had never done before. Never mind the fact that I had made the company tons of money! There wasn't any way that he would even consider that I might leave. I was his right-hand man, so to speak.

I then broke into my "I'll pay it back, it was my mistake" soliloquy. You guessed it, more laughing. He thought it was absurd. And I guess in a sense, maybe it was, although it seemed like the fair thing to do at the time. My boss reminded me that we all make mistakes.

Of course he was not going to accept my resignation with my history of helping to make the company profitable. Nor would he allow me to even suggest that I pay the company back. This was one secret we'd keep to ourselves he said, and otherwise it would be business as usual. He didn't need to ask me more questions, monitor my future negotiations, or even track how every little thing was going (all which I volunteered, since I obviously couldn't be trusted anymore). Again, he insisted that it was business as usual.

Now my boss was a very clever man and an incredible mentor. He went on to ask me what I would do if one of the people I supervised came to me in a similar situation. Obviously, I would never consider firing them. And quite frankly, if they helped make me look good, achieving and exceeding company goals, there was no question what I would do. I would tell them that accidents happen, and that we'd figure out a way to get past this together.

While answering my boss' questions I came to the realization that my initial reaction, thinking that I should just quit because I was no longer trustworthy, was extreme. This was a blatant example of how I would have been much kinder and gentler to someone else than I was to myself.

Often we hold ourselves to a higher standard than we would hold others. Time and time again, we punish ourselves for not being good enough, fast enough, rich enough, or thin enough. And yet, if someone else would do or say the same thing, we would be kind and supportive, patient and understanding. In short, sometimes we don't treat ourselves as well as we would our best friends.

EXERCISE 1: Would You Like to Forgive Yourself?

Grab your journal and take a few minutes to consider your past. Are you still beating yourself up for something you've said or done? Start by answering the following questions and write down whatever comes to mind. The next meditation provides an opportunity to forgive yourself and release any self-judgement relating to your past actions.

- Have you broken a promise to someone?

- Have you ever said or done something that you wish you had not?

- Did you do a mediocre job when you know you could've done better?

- Have you harmed or disrespected yourself or someone else?

- Did you forego an opportunity because you weren't courageous?

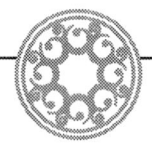

Self-Forgiveness Meditation: 14 minutes

Begin by closing your eyes. Take a deep breath in, and hold it. Exhaling very slowly, just relaxing and letting go of any tension, any tightness you might be holding in your body or your mind. And, another deep breath in, holding it as long as you comfortably can. And now, exhaling slowly and gently, becoming more and more relaxed with each breath. Just slowing down, and letting go. Breathing easily and gently, going deeper and deeper into a peaceful state of relaxation.

PAUSE 3 SECONDS . . .

CONTINUED ▶

And you know that you are perfectly safe here at this time. And no one and nothing can harm you. So you can just take your time to relax, let go, and unwind.

And you may begin to notice that your eyes are becoming comfortably closed. And your eyelids are starting to feel heavy. Heavy and so relaxed, calm and peaceful.

And a feeling of relaxation flows to your head and your face, as all the muscles in your head and face relax. Any tension or tightness is just beginning to melt away. You feel calm and peaceful, just like you do when you are about to drift off to sleep.

And now that gentle flow of relaxation moves into your shoulders and through your chest, as all the muscles of your shoulders and chest area relax. And that warm peaceful feeling flows down your arms and your back to the base of your spine, continuing down your legs all the way to the tips of your toes. Your mind is at ease and your entire body feels heavy, heavy and perfectly relaxed.

PAUSE 5 SECONDS...

Now begin to see yourself in the most serene and peaceful place imaginable. Maybe you are in a Japanese garden, by an open meadow, or next to a calm mountain lake. Whatever you imagine is perfect, just so long as you find it completely relaxing, comfortable, quiet, and calm.

This amazing place is an oasis of renewal, regeneration, and second chances. Here you can easily forgive yourself and transform the energy of self-doubt, disappointment, anger, or frustration back to pure love. Gently and gracefully you can let go of any restrictive feelings that no longer serve you, or that might be holding you back from loving yourself or living life to its fullest.

Now imagine you have a list of any circumstance when you said something you wished you could have taken back, or when

CONTINUED ▶

you had done something that was less than what you could have achieved. Any situation when you might not have lived up to your own expectations and all the names of people you might not have treated kindly with your words or actions, including yourself.

Although it may not have felt like it at the time, these experiences were truly a blessing. For without them, you might not have learned what you now know about yourself or the world around you. So take a moment now to honor these people and thank them for helping you discover more about yourself and about life. In your mind, imagine you are sending them love from your heart to theirs.

PAUSE 10 SECONDS . . .

And as you thank them and think about them with love, you begin to notice that there is a warm, beautiful white glow surrounding you now. It is as if you are in the center of the most loving and accepting place imaginable. There is some kind of transformation taking place inside of you now, and you feel blessed and free. It is like a heavy, heavy weight has been lifted off your shoulders and that feels good.

PAUSE 5 SECONDS . . .

And you may have noticed that there is a little ceremonial fountain not far from where you are now. The water in the fountain can transform everything that is written on your list and any other lingering effects of these words or actions, back to the essence of pure love. So when you are ready, place your list in the fountain.

PAUSE 3 SECONDS . . .

Good. And as the paper begins to dissolve, you notice you feel a little lighter, a little more relaxed and free.

CONTINUED ▶

PAUSE 3 SECONDS...

Now say to yourself, "I love you, and I forgive you wholly and completely."

PAUSE 5 SECONDS...

And as you watch your list melt away, you feel peaceful and content. Any unwanted feelings or emotions relating to those people or events that were trapped in your body have now been released and transformed into love. You have forgiven yourself and now you are truly free.

Feel yourself breathing more effortlessly now. Take a deep breath in, and experience what your body, mind, and spirit feel like now that you are free of the judgments you placed on yourself in the past. You remember now that you have choices about your actions, and from this point forward, you are becoming more in tune with your divine goodness and your true potential.

So take another moment or two to experience what it feels like to know that you are perfect and lovable just as you are.

PAUSE 5 SECONDS...

You have reawakened the most divine version of yourself, without judgment, expectation, anger, resentment, or bias holding you back anymore. You now know that from this point forward you can love yourself with kindness and compassion, understanding that everything in your life happens for a reason.

PAUSE 5 SECONDS...

And now as I count from three to one you will become more awake, more alert, and ready to live your life fully. Confident and filled with love.

CONTINUED ▶

3 . . . feeling full of natural vibrant energy,
2 . . . filled with joy and happiness, and
1 . . . eyes wide open, feeling good and ready to enjoy the rest of your day.

> ### Post Meditation
>
> 1. Practice going back to your special oasis, by closing your eyes and taking three deep breaths. Imagine returning to the place you visited in your meditation.
>
> 2. Take a few minutes now to write down ways you can remember to be kinder to yourself. How can you actively practice self-forgiveness so that you won't be burdened with carrying the weight of self-judgement in the future?
>
> #### Circle Discussion:
> Take 10-15 minutes in your Circle to talk about ways that you can be kinder to yourself. How can you remember to let go or forgive yourself for the past and move on?

EXERCISE 2: Your Dream Team

Your "Dream Team" is a group of real or fictional people who you can call on to give you an unbiased view of reality. They will be your imaginary consultants, ready at your whim, to help you recognize if you are treating yourself fairly with kindness and consideration or if you are blowing things out of proportion.

1. Let's start by imagining someone who loves you unconditionally. This might be your mother or father, grandparents, spouse, a friend, or someone fictional who honors and appreciates who you are. Write down their name under the heading, "My Dream Team."

2. Next, think of a wise person you admire. This can be someone you know or an individual you've read about somewhere. Choose someone who has achieved something great or worthy of respect. (Think Nelson Mandela, Gandhi, or Mother Theresa.) Add this name to your list.

3. Now imagine your version of the perfect parent or grandparent. This can be someone from a TV show or movie, your fairy godmother, or anyone else you can think of, real or imaginary. Write their name down if you know it or give them a name if you've made them up.

The names on your list are now your new Dream Team. Keep it someplace accessible so that you can easily turn to your team for advice.

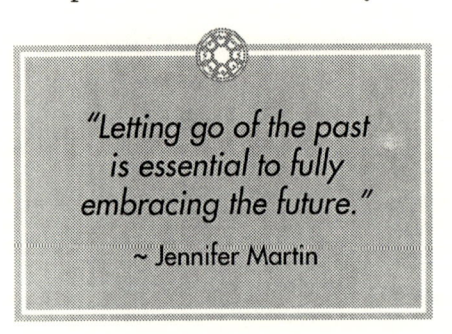

> *"Letting go of the past is essential to fully embracing the future."*
> ~ Jennifer Martin

The next time you find that you have said something or acted in a way you wished you hadn't, take a moment to check in with the team to see if you are being fair with yourself.

Imagine asking them for their honest feedback about how you are processing the after-effects of the situation. Let your Dream Team help keep you in check so that you don't carry around unnecessary baggage, feeling poorly about something you said or did in a manner that was out of proportion to the event.

Forgiving Yourself & Others

Has someone ever done something so terribly wrong to you that you didn't think you could forgive him or her? Or was there ever a point where you did or said something you felt was unforgivable? When you encounter these situations, what do you do? How do you forgive others, and even more importantly, how can you forgive yourself?

> ### Self-Forgiveness Ritual
>
> If you tend to beat yourself up, mercilessly going over and over in your mind what you did or said, what do you do to find balance again?
>
> Try this technique or create one of your own:
>
> 1. Take several deep breaths. Imagine breathing in white light of pure unconditional love.
>
> 2. Now imagine you are a coffee press. Each time you exhale, a screen pushes anything you no longer wish to keep from the top of your head out the bottom of your feet. As you breathe in, you refill with white light from the soles of your feet to the top of your head, completely cleansing and rejuvenating yourself from the inside out.
>
> 3. Continue the process until you feel peaceful, serene, and filled with love.

My Boyfriend Carl

I had a boyfriend who always said he would pick me up at 7:00 p.m. for our Friday night date and maybe one out of ten times he would be on time. More likely, he was an hour or two late, and sometimes he didn't show up at all.

As crazy as it might sound, I loved him, and over and over I forgave him. When we were together, my life felt complete. At these times, I could set aside all his broken promises and commitments; he was everything to me. I thought in my heart we were "meant to be."

Well as you can imagine, someone who was incapable of setting dates and arriving on time may also have had other shortcomings. This was the case with Carl. (Again, names have been changed to protect the lying, cheating, and chronically late).

Okay, so Carl didn't know how to love me in the way that I wanted. He struggled with keeping his commitments and following through on his promises. And oh yeah, although he was separated, he never got a divorce from the wife I found out about after the first time we slept together. Regardless, there was still something magical about our relationship and I was hooked, possibly addicted.

Without detailing the entire on-again off-again relationship that I was a part of for almost 5 years, I can just say that one day I realized that I had had enough. Finally I had hit my limit. It was the morning after one of our little rendezvous that he did something that made it perfectly clear to me I was neither loved nor respected. Or thankfully, at least that's the way it appeared to me at the time.

I called it quits and told Carl to never call me or see me again. I would no longer be available to him. I finally knew I deserved better.

As a result of my experience with Carl, my relationships did improve over time. I had resolved never to allow someone into my life romantically who wasn't really available, and from that point forward I kept true to my word.

I stopped seeing Carl, and then, I stopped taking his calls. However, for many years to come, I still held anger and resentment toward him. It seemed that even though he was physically out of my life, he would still occasionally pop into my thoughts.

No matter how much time went by, the thought of him stirred me. It was clear that even though I might never see him again, we were still very much connected. On some level, the magic between us was holding me back in my present relationships.

I realized that the ties between us needed to be completely severed. I knew that the only way I could let him go would be to acknowledge and honor the experience for what it was, forgive myself for my own participation, and release any underlying contracts between us.

Releasing Our Connection

Honoring the Experience

Instead of telling Carl about how much he hurt me, I recognized the need to tell him (in a letter that I would never send) how much I loved him. I knew that somehow feeling grateful rather than spiteful would help to free me.

I explained in the letter how much I enjoyed the time we had together, how alive I felt in his presence, and how connected I felt to him. I thanked him for loving me in the way he knew how and blessed him for teaching me so much about what was important to me in love relationships.

Self-Forgiveness

Next, I wrote another letter. This letter was addressed to the aspect of myself who doubted she could ever experience the same kind of love again. I wrote to that part of me who hung in there because she didn't believe she could do any better.

I told her how much I admired her and appreciated that she could love so passionately. I forgave her for not believing in herself more, for not knowing how to ask for what she wanted, and for not knowing she deserved to be loved as part of a reciprocal relationship. I blessed this part of myself and I vowed to always remember what I learned through my experience with Carl. I told her I would be cutting the strings that tied me to the pain, regret, anger, sadness, and all the feelings of failure of the past.

Cutting the Ties

The next thing that I did was make a list of any broken promises and any circumstances where I could remember one of us owed something (emotional, financial, spiritual, physical, etc.) to the other. I recorded absolutely anything relating to our relationship that I felt was out of balance or that I still experienced as an emotional charge.

After the list, I wrote a Karmic Release Contract that included our names, the date, and our "spiritual" agreement to release any "debts" owed to either one of us.

Saying Goodbye – The Ceremony

When I was done, I then created a special ceremony. I lit candles, said an invocation, and set an intention to cut the ties between us forever. I read out loud both the letters and the list I had written. Next, I read the Karmic Release Contract I created. When I had finished, I burned all the letters, the list, and the contract in my wastebasket.

Freedom from Carl

Although nothing seemed to change physically for me, on a deeper level I felt the ritual had served its purpose. There was some kind of shift, I just couldn't put my finger on it. Sometime later, a friend asked me if I had heard from Carl lately, and it was then that I noticed I had changed. There was a part of me that still reminisced about our relationship, but I didn't have an energetic charge attached to it anymore. It felt like all the air had been released from that emotional balloon. I was free.

Releasing the baggage of past relationships doesn't have to be difficult. Letting go of these energetic ties can enhance your ability to experience the most satisfying love life possible.

A Karma Primer

If you aren't familiar with the term karma, it can be understood as a universal mirror that reflects our own words, actions, thoughts, and beliefs back to us so that we might see and experience who we are and what we do from a different perspective (and hopefully learn from it).

There really isn't good or bad karma; it is a completely nonjudgmental process that just reflects what it sees back to you. So if you help out an elderly neighbor, you might expect to receive help yourself sometime. And likewise, if you scream nasty names at your ex, you might see something similar show up in this life (or in a future life), as well.

When we interact with others, particularly in love relationships, we often establish karmic debts or ties that are left unresolved. This is part of the reason why it becomes easy to continue repeating the same patterns over and over again. Often, the same scene keeps playing in your mirror until you are ready to break the tie and end the cycle.

The bottom line is that whatever you do in your life, the karma mirror will play back to you. If you treat others with kindness and consideration, this is, in general, what you will receive back. So when it comes to karma, the Golden Rule really is golden; do unto others as you would have them do unto you.

EXERCISE 3: Releasing an Emotionally Charged Relationship

If there is someone from your past or in your life presently who you would like to let go of once and for all, complete the following steps.

1. **What is Holding You Back?**
   When you have someone in mind, write down their name in your journal at the top of the page. Then consider if there is anything holding you back from letting this person go. Record any thoughts or feelings you have.

2. **What's the Value of Holding on to this Relationship?**
   There must be some reason that you have kept the fire alive, so to speak. For some reason, staying connected holds value to you. If you know what that "gain" might be, write it down. Do your best not to judge it, just acknowledge it.

3. **Write a Love Letter to the Person You Are Releasing**
   Now, write a love letter or a letter of appreciation to this person. This is not something to send, it is just a way of acknowledging the relationship on a positive note. Think of what you learned through the experience and anything you enjoyed about your relationship.

4. **A Letter Forgiving Yourself**
   Next, write a letter to any part of yourself that you haven't forgiven. Be willing to forgive yourself for not believing that you deserved to have better, for saying or doing things that you know weren't done in the most loving way, or for choosing to be in the relationship at all. Include whatever feels appropriate for you personally.

5. **Record Your History Together**
   Make a list of any unpaid debts (physical, emotional, spiritual, financial, etc.) or unfilled promises that took place during or after your relationship together. Note any time when one of you might have felt that something was "owed" to the other. Record any circumstances when there was an inequality with give and take, when one person was unfair or harmed the other, or anything else that was out of balance in either party's favor.

6. Releasing All Contracts

The next step is a Karmic Release, an opportunity to wipe the slate clean. The words you use are not as essential as the feelings and intentions you have for creating this change in your life. This contract can cut the ties between you. Make something up or use the sample on the following page.

7. Special Ceremony

The final step is having a special ceremony to honor and release the past once and for all. You can say a special prayer, sing, dance, plant a tree, or create a wish list for your future. I suggest at a minimum you read aloud everything you have written in this exercise. Decide how you will (safely) dispose of the letters when you are done. Include in your ceremony anything that feels exactly right for you as you let go of the past and confidently move on to something better.

An Overview of Releasing an Emotionally Charged Relationship

1. Write a thank you note to the person or circumstance involved, acknowledging what you gained or learned from the experience. (This is for your own growth, not for them. Do not send it or give it to them.)

2. Write a note forgiving that part of yourself who perhaps didn't know better, chose the situation (on some level), or participated in some way consciously or unconsciously.

3. Make a list of anything between you that was left out of balance or that still carries an emotional charge for you. Then, write a contract of past, present, and future karmic release, recognizing anything you can remember that tied the two of you together.

4. Create a ceremony of your choosing to release everything. Read everything you've written aloud and decide how you will (safely) dispose of your letters.

Karmic Release Contract

On today's date, _____, and in all time, space, and dimensions in the past, present, or future, including parallel universes, I, (your name) _____, also known as (any other names you have gone by in the past)_____, hereby cancel and dissolve any and all contracts that may have been made or will be made tying me in any way to the person I know in this life as (their name) _____.

I give great thanks to (their name) _____ for the relationship we shared, and for what I learned from our experience together. I hereby cancel and dissolve any karmic debts, ties, or contracts known or unknown that we have consciously or unconsciously made with one another. I completely release you from any obligations you have to me and I ask your higher spirit to release me of any obligations I have to you.

If there is anything I must do in order to fully dissolve the karmic ties between us, I ask that this information be presented to me in a clear and gentle way within the next 24 hours. Otherwise, no other action shall be needed to complete this karmic release.

(Their name) _____, I thank you, bless you, honor you, and release you forever. I now sever the energetic ties we have created in body, mind, and spirit. We are no longer bound to each other in any time, place, or dimension. Any interaction we may have from this point forward will be without the energetic effects of the past, present, or future.

It is done, it is done, it is done.

Signed: _____   _____
                Signature   Date

Note: This agreement is only for you. There is no need to send it or share it with the person you are releasing. If within 24 hours you receive some indication of something that you need to do in order to be released, follow your intuition. When you have completed anything left undone, begin the contract process again.

COMMUNICATION TIPS

💬 The Value of a Balanced Apology

Clearly, no one likes to admit that they were wrong, mistaken, or could have done or said something better. But I think we would all agree that if more people took responsibility for their actions, many arguments would never take place. Admitting your shortcomings in your love relationship is not a sign of weakness. Rather, it is an opportunity to reconnect with your partner.

Most people rarely learn the finer points of giving and receiving an apology. In a perfect world, both parties would honestly share their feelings until some kind of resolution is reached. Ideally, each person would listen to the other, and the receiver would acknowledge what was said, regardless of whether or not they feel they can forgive.

💬 Preparing to Ask for Forgiveness

It is never too late to say, "I'm sorry." By using the following techniques to prepare for your apology (or any other potentially challenging dialogue), you can dramatically impact the outcome of your interaction. Start by taking a few minutes to practice your apology out loud before you communicate with someone else. Knowing what you intend to say beforehand will give you confidence and help you acheive your desired result.

See the Other Person's Perspective

Find a quiet spot and imagine the person to whom you would like to apologize. Now see yourself stepping into their body and imagine what their thoughts or feelings might have been during the situation at hand. Give yourself a minute or two to really sense what they might have been feeling when this incident occurred. Allow their perspective to help you become more sensitive to their needs when you make your apology. The more you can do to understand and prepare to respond to their needs before you apologize, the better your chances of success will be.

📑 How to Apologize

When you are ready to say you're sorry, remember to:

1. Make eye contact and speak slowly and clearly.

2. Be sincere. Choose only words that genuinely reflect your feelings. If you don't feel it, don't say it. The idea here is to establish trust.

3. Take responsibility for your actions. You don't need to apologize for your feelings though. It's okay to be angry, sad, mad, frustrated, or happy. Your emotions do not require any apology. However, if while you were mad you punched a hole in the wall, apologizing for your actions (the hole in the wall) would be appropriate.

4. Let your partner know why you are apologizing. For example, "I feel badly that I said some unkind things to you. I love you and I want to work this out."

5. Share your honest feelings about them and your relationship together. "I hope that we are still in love 50 years from now."

6. Give your partner the opportunity to share their feelings too: "Is there anything that you would like to share with me?" If your partner has something to say, do your best to:

    - Remain calm. You are in the driver's seat. It's your job to keep the conversation going in a positive direction.

    - Be a good listener and acknowledge what they are saying. Let them know you are listening (even if you don't agree).

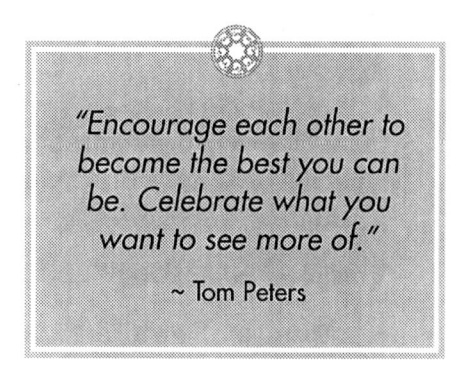

    - Resist the temptation to argue. Stay focused on saying your piece, listening to your partner, and moving forward with the rest of your relationship.

> *"Encourage each other to become the best you can be. Celebrate what you want to see more of."*
>
> ~ Tom Peters

7. Ask if there is anything that you can do to help or to make amends. For example, "Is there anything that I can do to help us get past this?" or, "Can I replace the vase I broke?"

8. Stay open to the possibilities. Have the best case scenario in mind, but don't walk away if someone isn't ready to forgive you. Be willing to allow them time to process their own feelings.

💬 How to Receive an Apology

When someone extends their apology, do your best to:

1. Stay calm. If you value the relationship, try to maintain a constructive emotional state even if the event or the apology brings up some challenging feelings.

2. Be a good listener. Give the person making the apology a chance to fully explain their position without interruption. Keep in mind it may have taken them a lot of courage to speak with you.

3. Remember that you have a choice. You can choose to accept their apology and forgive them, or just listen to what they say. *You are not required to tell them it is okay if it is not.*

4. If you are given an opportunity to share your feelings, be honest, even if you feel upset by the person's actions or choices.

5. If you share your side, use "I feel" messages to tell them how you feel instead of blaming them for what they did. Better yet, let them know what you wish they would do the next time something similar came up, so that they'll be clear what you would like in the future.

Example of an Apology Dialogue:

Jim: "Wendy, I'm sorry I was late to your sister's wedding. I didn't intend to arrive after the ceremony started. I know that there isn't any good excuse for my actions. I just wasn't paying attention to the time. I love you. I didn't mean to be disrespectful to you or your family.

FORGIVENESS & LETTING GO OF THE PAST

              Would you be willing to forgive me? I don't want this big mistake to ruin the rest of our relationship."

Wendy: "Jim, I appreciate your apology, *and* I don't think you had any idea of how important it was to me that you were there on time. Especially since I was in the wedding and everyone saw you come in late! I want to forgive you, but I don't think that I can right now. We're just going to have to wait and see how things pan out."

Jim: "Honey, I love you so much. I understand why you are upset and I promise I'll try to be more aware of your feelings in the future. Is there anything that I could do that could help us get through this?"

Wendy: "I don't know. But every time that you are late I feel completely disrespected. I feel like you don't care about me or our relationship. I hate when you forget me. I wish that you would be more respectful of my time."

> *"We don't see things as they are, we see them as we are."*
> ~ Anais Nin

Jim: "Honey, you are very important to me. I'm going to try my best to be on time and be respectful to you in the future. What if anytime I keep you waiting, you can completely rule over me for that same amount of time. If I'm ten minutes late, you can tell me to do anything for ten minutes. Taking out the trash or anything else you'd like. Would you be open to giving something like this a try?"

Wendy: "I guess I would be willing to give your idea a shot, *and* what I really want is for you to be on time."

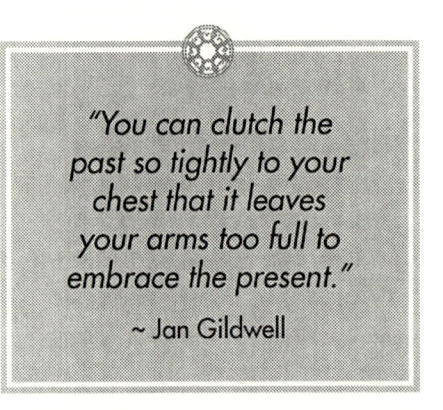

> *"You can clutch the past so tightly to your chest that it leaves your arms too full to embrace the present."*
>
> ~ Jan Gildwell

EXERCISE 4: Saying "I'm Sorry"

Let's practice saying, "I'm sorry," and receiving an apology. Find a partner or practice on your own in front of the mirror. One person will apologize and the other person will be the receiver. (If you are doing this by yourself, you can play both parts.) You can try one of the scenarios below or use real-life situations. If you would like to practice for future apology, tell your partner about the circumstance and the role they will be playing.

When you've completed a scenario, switch roles so that each person can have a chance to give and receive an apology. Your goal is to come to some kind of resolution each time. Continue to exchange thoughts and feelings until some type of agreement can be reached. Keep in mind the end result might be simply agreeing to disagree.

Possible Scenarios:

- I'm sorry, I forgot to _____.
  For example: I'm sorry I forgot to pick you up on time.

- I'm sorry for keeping _____ a secret from you.

- I'm sorry for being insensitive to/about _____.

- I'm sorry for not honoring our agreement to _____.

EXERCISE 5: Forgiveness Affirmations

Learning to forgive yourself can be a great blessing. Use the following affirmations or create your own:

- I am graceful and whole just as I am.

- Every situation in my life offers me an opportunity to grow in clarity and purpose.

- I am a reflection and expression of divine perfection.

- Each and every day I learn and grow from my experiences; each interaction is perfect in its own way.

- When I say, "I'm sorry," I set my spirit free. When I honor every aspect of who I am, I open myself to greater love.

Make Your Weekly Commitments

Choose a step from your Action List (from Chapter 2) that you will complete this week to make progress toward your relationship goals. Also, spend some time doing "something wonderful" just for you.

Practice & Review

Have opportunities presented themselves for you to practice some of what you've learned in the past few weeks? Remember that it is okay to say, "no," when you don't want to do something or when complying with someone's request wouldn't allow you to honor your own boundaries. Also, keep your "but" to yourself and use an "and" to connect a respectful acknowledgement of the other person's opinion (or request) with what feels right for you. If you can't seem to let go of your negative judgements about your words or actions, check in with your Dream Team for some honest advice. And don't forget that it's never too late to take responsibility for anything you've done with an honest apology. Wherever you find yourself, recognize how far you've come. You're amazing! Keep up the good work!

> **Tip of the Week:**
> Holding on to the past requires a great deal of time and energy. If you were to let go, how would you spend your newfound time differently?

FOR CIRCLE MEMBERS

Week 5 Homework:
Complete prior to attending your 5th Circle
- Read Chapter 6
- Do Exercises 1, 2, & 4
- Complete your weekly commitments

Bring to the Meeting:
- Your *More Love, More Joy!* book
- A journal/notebook and a pen/pencil
- Art supplies for Exercise 3 (see pg. 117 for full list): poster board, markers, pens, magazines, etc.

In Your Circle You Will Complete:
- Exercises 3
- Meditation

6

Learning to Honor Receiving

"The real voyage of discovery consists not in seeking new landscapes, but in having new eyes."
~ Marcel Proust

Most of us grow up learning that it is far better to give than to receive. Society drills this message into us through religion, etiquette books, television, the girl or boy scouts, magazines, and advice columns. In my experience, it became clear very early on that everyone who knew best knew that giving was the "right" thing to do.

I'm not knocking religion or people more refined than myself, but I wonder if this logic is why so many of us wind up feeling bad or guilty about what we have (unless of course we give some or all of it away). Could this have anything to do with why we put others' needs far ahead of our own? Could this be why financial prosperity is only experienced by a select few?

Receiving is actually an essential part of the complete cycle of exchange. Unfortunately, many of us have never learned that being a good receiver can be equally as worthwhile as the giving itself.

My History with Giving and Receiving

My grandfather died when I was 7 and left my grandmother with a meager life insurance policy, a little cash, and a car. She had never worked, and now it looked like she might have to get a job to survive.

Before he died, my grandfather convinced my father that it was his duty to care for his mother. Therefore, being the only son, my father at 28-years-old, now had another mouth to feed. He moved my grandmother into a smaller apartment and agreed to help her. She could pretty much carry on her life, business as usual.

Unfortunately, my grandmother was a card player, a gambler, and a pretty compulsive one at that. I don't have many memories of her in our lives except for the times when she came around to beg money from my father (her son) to help bail her out (again) of some financial mess she created. It seemed that no matter what my father did to help my grandmother, she somehow managed to whittle it away.

> "It's choice—not chance—that determines your destiny."
> ~ Jean Nidetch

While everyone I knew was being programmed that it was better to give than receive, I also learned that as a child you became indebted to your parents forever. It seemed that since your parents had done something generous by raising you, you owed them (money for rent, money to get their car out of hock, money to replace anything that they had gambled away). In other words, if someone gave you their love and caring, it could come back to bite you in the wallet over and over again.

Regardless of what each of our individual stories might be about giving and receiving, I have found that most people have never really learned how to receive (to say nothing of learning how to be a good giver). When someone compliments us on our haircut, our clothing, or our new car, the first thing we've been taught to do is downplay it. "Really, I think they cut it a little too short," or, "Oh, this old thing?" For whatever reason, many of us don't even know how to take a compliment, let alone a gift or a gesture of kindness.

Personally, I found myself in my mid-20s knowing very little about how to accept common consideration, a compliment, or even a gift from a friend. In other words, I was a really crappy receiver. In my dysfunctional little world, I became certain that if I didn't allow someone to do anything for me, I could avoid owing something they would never stop collecting (such as money, attention, sex, etc.).

I would never allow a date to pay for dinner and I always insisted on buying anything that anyone (even my parents) offered. I was uncomfortable with compliments and couldn't be bothered with someone opening the door for me. I was determined to take care of myself and owe nothing.

Needless to say, something was wrong. I never really let people care for me out of fear that I might owe them something if I accepted their gifts. It wasn't surprising that I wasn't involved in very balanced relationships. I had been giving away for a long time, yet I wasn't feeling very good about myself. Regardless of all I heard and learned, it didn't feel like giving was better than receiving. I knew that something was definitely missing.

Learning to Receive

I have received several unusual messages from people I call "angels" in my life. This is one of those stories. One day, my car broke down and I took the bus home from the repair shop. It was rush hour and if you were able to sit down, you were lucky. After a few stops, I was fortunate enough to see two seats open up just to my left. As I slid into one, a very smelly babbling homeless woman sat down into the seat next to me. Although I wasn't crazy about sitting next to someone I thought at the time was a stinky nut, I was happy to be seated for my long ride home.

I tried for several stops not to make eye contact with this woman, which was a challenge as she was just chatting away and everyone could clearly see she was speaking directly to me. I felt uncomfortable because I definitely didn't know her and I had no idea what she wanted.

> *"You can explore the universe looking for somebody who is more deserving of your love and affection than you are, and you will not find that person anywhere."*
>
> ~ Buddhist Expression

I did my best to stay relaxed and detached but as soon as she raised her voice and started in on me again, I couldn't help but listen.

"You know what's wrong with you don't you? Your problem is that you don't honor receiving. You have no idea how to receive. You can't even accept a compliment for a job well done. You love being able to do nice things for people. It makes you feel good. Why would you want to deny someone else that pleasure? If you don't allow people to be nice to you and give to you, you don't allow them the pleasure of giving. You don't HONOR RECEIVING!"

She rambled on like this for what felt like a lifetime in a tone so loud I was certain that people on the street could hear what she was saying. I felt sure that every person on the bus and maybe a few in the general vicinity knew *my problem*. So there I sat for about 20 grueling minutes with sweat forming on my upper lip as I endured her wrath while pretending she was completely batty. The worst part was, I knew that she *was* talking to me. I did my best not to break into tears, all the while praying that she wouldn't somehow yell my name. Then I would be busted for sure.

So there it was: an angel message sent to me through the body of a homeless woman. And, it was a message that actually sounded like it had merit. I decided it would be worthwhile to start giving the whole thing some thought. After quite a bit of self-reflection, I finally came up with an image that helped it all make sense for me.

The Cycle of Giving and Receiving

Think of a clock. When you send out a compliment or give a gift, the energy of that gesture originates at 12:00 and continues to move clockwise around the center. If you tell a friend that she looks nice today, the energy goes from 12:00 towards 6:00 as she starts to register what you just said. At 6:00, she starts to affect the process. She says to you. "Really? This old thing?"

Then it happens, inside you on some deep level, you register rejection and the energy of your compliment reverses direction, ending up right back where you started at 12:00 (see Figure 6.1). Your intention of giving (or loving) has been cut off at the knees.

LEARNING TO HONOR RECEIVING 107

ENERGY FLOW OF A REJECTED COMPLIMENT

Circle is not completed because the energy ends up back at the starting point

When a compliment is given, energy begins to flow clockwise from 12:00

Compliment is downplayed and energy reverses direction

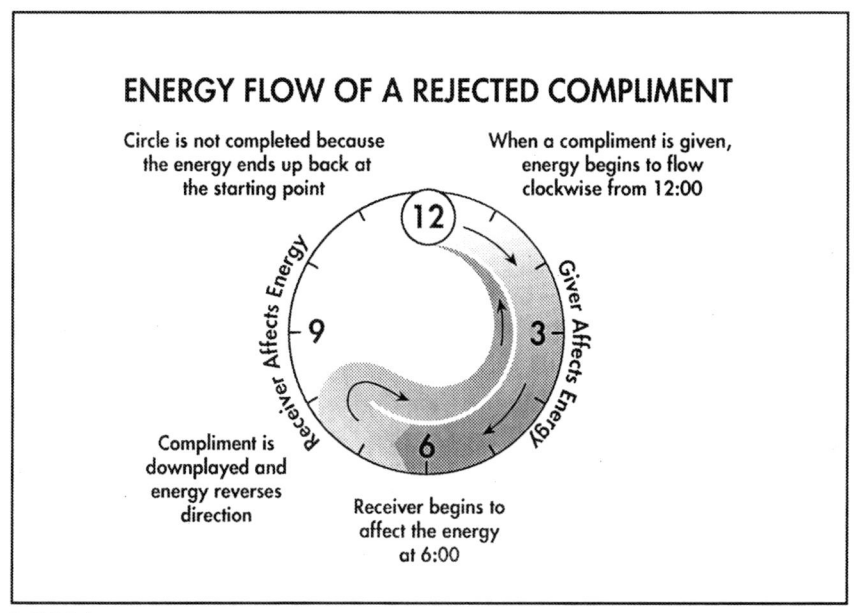

Receiver begins to affect the energy at 6:00

FIGURE 6.1

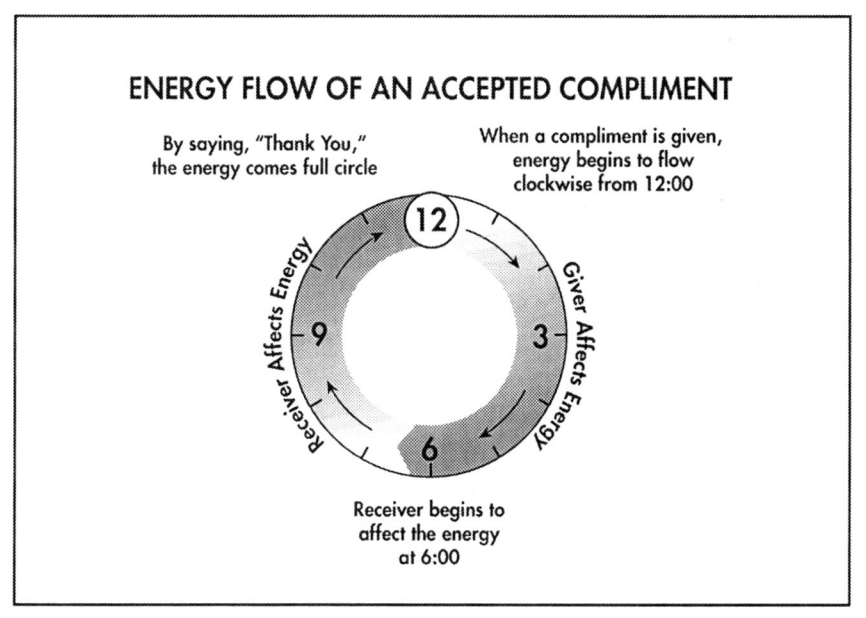

ENERGY FLOW OF AN ACCEPTED COMPLIMENT

By saying, "Thank You," the energy comes full circle

When a compliment is given, energy begins to flow clockwise from 12:00

Receiver begins to affect the energy at 6:00

FIGURE 6.2

Had your friend responded with a simple, "Thank you," she would have validated and acknowledged your loving intention and energetically completed the cycle all the way around the clock (see Figure 6.2). Both giving and receiving play an equally important part in the cycle of exchange.

Accepting Generosity

I recently talked to a hairdresser friend of mine, Molly, who was having a difficult time receiving money (tips, fair prices for services, etc.) from her clients. I asked Molly to imagine that one of her clients felt so excited about her new haircut or color that this woman reached out to give her a big hug. When I asked Molly how she would feel about this gesture, she said that a hug would be a perfect example of how her clients could show their love and appreciation for her services. She wished that every client responded this way. Molly considered a hug to be even more valuable than money, even if it wouldn't pay the rent.

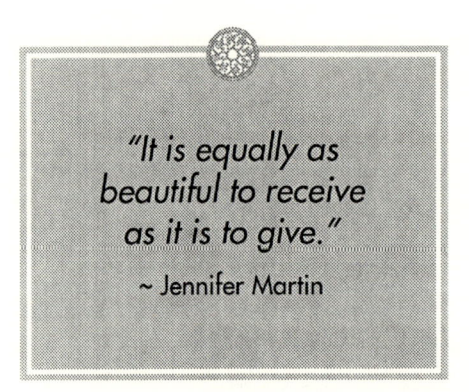

> *"It is equally as beautiful to receive as it is to give."*
> ~ Jennifer Martin

Next I asked, what if the same happy client reached out to hug her with excitement and instead of embracing her, Molly responded by taking a big step back and saying, "NO! Don't touch me." Molly couldn't even imagine doing anything so rude.

Of course, this is quite an extreme reaction towards someone who just wanted to show her appreciation. However, on a more subtle level, I explained that this is what happens when we don't say thank you, when we deny someone's offer to buy us lunch, reject a compliment, or even refuse payment for the work we do.

EXERCISE 1: Create Your Receiving Log

Notice and write down when someone:

- Opens the door for you.
- Bends down to pick up something that you dropped.
- Offers to take your shopping cart back to the store.
- Buys you lunch.
- Brings you a gift.
- Offers you her seat.
- Asks if he could help you.

What other ways have people been generous to you this week? How did you respond? Is there anything you could have done differently to honor their giving with heartfelt appreciation?

The Transformation (Learning to Receive Continued)

After meeting my "angel" on the bus, I knew that honoring receiving had merit. I recognized that I was an "over-giver," or at least that was the term my therapist gave it. I was great, maybe even exceptional, at giving. I was wildly generous with others. Not a meal went by with a friend that I didn't insist on paying. I was always offering to drive, even going out of my way to pick everyone up. If someone had a problem to solve, I was their girl. Over and over I proved that I could take care of myself, my friends, and my family (while enabling a few of them). There was nothing that I couldn't do, pay for, or provide.

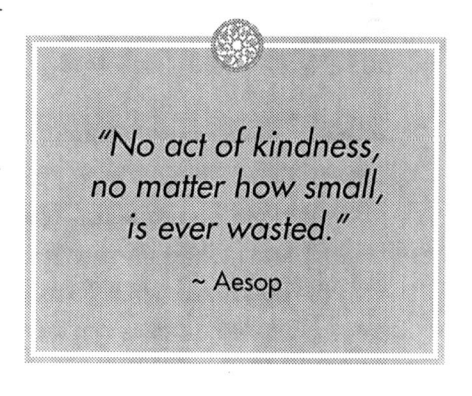

> *"No act of kindness, no matter how small, is ever wasted."*
> ~ Aesop

I hadn't put my finger on it at the time, but I was actually trying not to owe anyone anything. And, by that same logic, I was indebting other people to me, while all along looking like the hero.

I knew in my heart that I was full of crap. This whole over-giving thing went much deeper. When I was doing all the giving and taking care of others, I wasn't letting anyone into my life emotionally. As much as I knew I could take care of myself, I wasn't allowing friends, family, lovers, or partners to truly be in a reciprocal relationship. I recognized that what I was doing wasn't "healthy," and it probably had a lot to do with why there always seemed to be something missing from my life.

The homeless woman on the bus kept coming to mind. I knew that she was on target. Right then and there I made a commitment to myself. For the next 30 days I was going to practice receiving (and practice giving up some of the control).

I wrote a message and taped it to my bathroom mirror, my steering wheel, and over my driver's license picture in my wallet. Yellow sticky notes were everywhere screaming, "I HONOR RECEIVING." It became my mantra. I was intent on being equally as good at receiving as I was at giving. Baby steps, I told myself. Maybe this was what was missing in my life?

> *"A compliment is a gift, not to be thrown away carelessly, unless you want to hurt the giver."*
> ~ Eleanor Hamilton

Whenever I dropped a pencil by someone else's foot I took a breath and instead of diving toward their toes with a vengeance, I thought, "I honor receiving," and did my best to allow them to get to the pencil first. I practiced saying, "thank you," no matter what I felt (or heard) inside. With practice (and numerous deep breaths) I was determined to learn how to graciously receive.

If I was invited to lunch or out on a date and the other person said that they wanted to pay, instead of aggressively grabbing the check and forcing my credit card on the waiter, I managed to say, "Thank you, I hope that you will let me buy next time."

What I noticed was that just like me, these people really didn't want something from me. They just wanted to be nice. Sending a compliment or buying a gift or lunch didn't have an agenda most of the time.

Now, many years later, I find that I am a much better receiver than I used to be. I can take a compliment and even accept very generous gifts far better than I used to (although I may go on thanking people much longer than necessary so I'm certain that the giver really understands how much their generosity means to me). I find that even with work, I am becoming continually better at believing that I am worth it as I receive payment for the services I offer with thanks and appreciation.

I wish I could re-write what society tells us, that it is equally as beautiful to receive as it is to give. My hope would be that you will continue to give when you are guided to or feel the urge to do so, that you learn to honor receiving, and that either act be based in love and equal exchange. (For more about equal exchange see pg. 112.)

COMMUNICATION TIPS

🗩 Show Your Appreciation

When someone says or does something you like, remember to let them know that you appreciate their kindness. A simple, "thank you," confirms for the giver that their gesture positively affected you. If you enjoyed what you received, be sure to let them know that they are appreciated, and you would be open to seeing it happen again. This kind of communication positively reinforces behavior you like and increases the chances that it will reoccur. This week, see if you can recognize someone for a job well done.

🗩 Being a Good Receiver

Learning to accept a compliment (or a gift) is equally as important as learning how to give one. The best way you can pay your respect and appreciation to someone who has treated you with kindness is to accept a compliment by saying, "thank you."

Regardless of any urge you might have to downplay their words or actions, from this point forward, practice sharing how much their compliment or gift meant to you, and say, "thank you."

EXERCISE 2: Saying "Thank You"

This week, practice receiving a compliment or the generosity of others with a simple, "thank you." Do your best to accept the compliment or positively acknowledge their gesture.

Universal Balance and Equal Exchange

Simply defined, equal exchange is fair trade in total harmony with the universe. If you haven't heard of this phrase before, it relates to an agreement that whatever is traded (i.e., time, money, love, etc.) will be exchanged for something that is perceived as being equally beneficial for everyone involved. A relationship based on the spirit of equal exchange exudes balance because something that feels of equal value is both given and received by each party, completing the cycle of giving in both directions.

In a love relationship based on equal exchange, one partner might make the meals while the other does the dishes afterwards. Another couple might exchange cleaning the bathrooms for doing the yard work or sex for a massage. If the balance of time, energy, or money feels fair to each party, then it is an equal exchange. In a long term relationship, it is not necessary to keep track of each individual exchange so much as intend to (in action and practice) stay in balance with the energy that is given and received by each person.

When we talk about equal exchange in business, it's in a sense like a barter. If a massage therapist agrees to provide a back massage to someone based on the principle of equal exchange, he or she would agree to receive whatever "gift" from the exchanger that the therapist perceives as being equal or desirable. This might be a time for time trade with a graphic designer, some veggies from the garden, a gift of the exchanger's choice, or $100. Equal exchange can be completely independent of what the free market might bring financially for goods or services.

The Cycle of Giving & Receiving Meditation: 12 minutes

Begin by closing your eyes. Take a deep breath in, and hold it. Exhaling very slowly, just relaxing and letting go of any tension, any tightness you might be holding in your body or your mind. And, another deep breath in, holding it as long as you comfortably can. And now, exhaling slowly and gently, becoming more and more relaxed with each breath. Just slowing down, and letting go. Breathing easily and gently, going deeper and deeper into a peaceful state of relaxation.

PAUSE 3 SECONDS...

And you know that you are perfectly safe here at this time. And no one and nothing can harm you. So you can just take your time to relax, let go, and unwind. And you may begin to notice that your eyes are becoming comfortably closed. And your eyelids are starting to feel heavy. Heavy and so relaxed, calm and peaceful.

And a feeling of relaxation flows to your head and your face, as all the muscles in your head and face relax. Any tension or tightness is just beginning to melt away. You feel calm and peaceful, just like you do when you are about to drift off to sleep.

And now that gentle flow of relaxation moves into your shoulders and through your chest, as all the muscles of your shoulders and chest area relax. And that warm peaceful feeling flows down your arms and your back, to the base of your spine, down your legs all the way to the tips of your toes. Your mind is at ease and your entire body feels heavy, heavy and perfectly relaxed.

PAUSE 5 SECONDS...

Now imagine that you have just experienced the perfect day off. You are calm and rested and you are now enjoying some quiet

CONTINUED ▶

time in your favorite place to relax. And you notice that you have been joined by an angel, an enlightened master. And there is something very peaceful about this being, and in their presence you feel loved.

PAUSE 3 SECONDS . . .

Your guide has come today to take you on a magic carpet ride where you will have a chance to observe the balance of giving and receiving. You'll activate your own ability to embrace gifts from others, and expand your potential to give and receive love. As you sit down upon the magic carpet, you become filled with a peaceful sense of serenity. The carpet begins to move slowly and gently and you feel perfectly peaceful and excited about this adventure.

PAUSE 3 SECONDS . . .

When you arrive at your first destination, you find yourself observing two co-workers. A woman approaches her associate and tells him that he has done a great job on their last project. As she is speaking, you become aware that you can see the light of her spirit glowing within her. As you watch her compliment her associate, her light begins to burn more brightly, and you can tell that she feels good about letting him know that he is appreciated.

When the man responds, instead of down-playing the compliment, he simply says, "thank you." And you can see that he also feels good about receiving the compliment, and a stream of the light within him extends itself out to his associate. When the two lights connect, you can feel a sense of love at its most divine essence growing within each of them as a result of this conversation.

CONTINUED ▶

Your guide explains that what you have observed was a complete energetic exchange that expanded both people's individual ability to receive more love, more kindness, and consideration into their lives. And your guide would like for you to see a little more about how this works.

As your carpet ride continues, you watch as one person holds open a door for someone else, and again, when a "thank you" is spoken, each person's light grows larger. Next, you observe two friends who are out to lunch. As they get ready to pay the bill, one friend offers to buy lunch for the other. When this gesture of kindness is extended and the friend accepts lunch by saying, "thank you," you can see that the light within each of them is expanding. At your last stop a woman is giving a massage therapist a big tip following her massage. As the masseuse says, "thank you," and gives her client a big hug, you can see that again, an equal exchange has taken place, and both of them feel blessed, as their lights shine more brightly from within.

As you leave the last scene, you become aware that you have just witnessed something very important. Your guide explains that all living things are connected to each other, we are all one. When you do something kind for someone else, you are also doing something wonderful for yourself. When you allow someone to give you a gift, or a compliment, or to treat you with kindness, you are honoring your love for yourself and reaffirming to the world that you are worthy of being loved. When you acknowledge a gift or gesture by saying "thank you," you are energetically sending love back to the giver and honoring their gift. In a very subtle way, you are allowing both of your lives' to be enhanced.

Your guide explains that it is now time for you to head home. And on the way you will be activating within you the ability to truly honor and embrace receiving, and enhance your personal power to attract more love, kindness, and consideration

CONTINUED ▶

into your life. As you lie down, you begin to notice your own light radiating from your heart. And your entire being starts to gently vibrate with soothing love energy. Every atom and molecule within you is gently expanding to increase your capacity for love.

PAUSE 3 SECONDS...

And now as the vibrations begin to subside, you recognize that something inside of you has shifted, and it feels wonderful now that you know, you are truly worthy of receiving love. So take just a moment to give thanks for what you have learned and for the activation which has expanded your potential to experience more love, kindness, and consideration into your life.

PAUSE 10 SECONDS...

And now as I count from three to one you will become more awake, more alert, and ready to live your life fully. Confident and filled with love.

3...feeling full of natural vibrant energy,
2...filled with joy and happiness, and
1... eyes wide open, feeling good and ready to enjoy the rest of your day.

Post Meditation

Write in your journal about how you can remember to honor receiving or how your ideas about giving and receiving may have changed.

Circle Discussion:

Share in your Circle about the ways you can remember to honor receiving or how your ideas about giving and receiving may have changed.

EXERCISE 3: Create a Visual Reminder to Honor Receiving
Get out your crayons, your colored pens, the glitter glue, your notebook, or anything else that will help you to be creative in your own unique way.

You'll be making something that represents and reminds you of the most evolved part of yourself, the part that knows how to honor receiving. This is the part of you that truly understands universal balance and knows how being a good receiver allows you to become a part of something much bigger than yourself.

EXERCISE 4: Affirmations to Honor Receiving
Develop the mantra, "I Honor Receiving, I Honor Receiving, I Honor Receiving..." Remind yourself of the beautiful gift that you give to others when you receive graciously. Recognize the intent of the giver and allow them the great pleasure of caring for you and loving you.

- I Honor Receiving.
- When I receive graciously, I am truly blessed.
- Honoring receiving is a beautiful way of loving the giver.

Make Your Weekly Commitments
Choose a step from your Action List (from Chapter 2) that you will complete this week to make progress toward your relationship goals. Also, spend some time doing "something wonderful" just for you.

> ### Tip of the Week:
> Be mindful of the way you interact with others this week. If you imagine that there is a giving and receiving scale, are you in balance? Love yourself by honoring receiving.

FOR CIRCLE MEMBERS

Week 6 Homework:
Complete prior to attending your 6th Circle
- Read Chapter 7
- Do Exercises 1 & 2
- Complete your weekly commitments

Bring to the Meeting:
- Your *More Love, More Joy!* book
- A journal/notebook and a pen/pencil
- A friend, colleague, or acquaintance for your *More Love, More Joy!* Miracle Networking Gathering
- 1-3 ideas of what you would like to add to (or subtract from) your life

In Your Circle You Will Complete:
- Meditation
- Miracle Networking Gathering

7

Creating a Life You'll Love

*"If you can imagine it, you can create it.
If you can dream it, you can become it."*
~ William Arthur Ward

Some people plan on annual visits to Hawaii, become the first person in their family to graduate from college, or drive their dream car. Meanwhile, others wait to be asked out for a date, never leave their dead-end job, or believe that doing what others tell them to do is better than deciding for themselves.

Manifesting the life of your dreams or the love life you've always wanted has everything to do with participation. The extent that you participate in your life is entirely up to you. No matter who you are or what you have done in the past, you always have choices. Choices about whom you date, where you go to college (if you choose to go), where you live, whom you marry, if you marry, whether to have children, or to work at a job you love. Of course, your chances of actually doing the things you want are much better if you actively make choices in pursuit of those goals.

If each little thought or action you took brought your dreams one step closer, what could you do right now to start making a change in your life?

How a Fortune Cookie Changed My Life

I had a job years ago that was extremely stressful. I negotiated real estate contracts on behalf of a very large corporation and frequently I was the messenger of difficult news. The contracts I negotiated could be worth thousands, hundreds of thousands, or even millions of dollars. As you can imagine, with such large amounts of money at stake, people would often allow the stress to drive them to do and say some pretty crazy things. I was called nasty four-letter words on a daily basis, verbally threatened almost monthly, followed home more than once, and twice was threatened with a gun.

During the early '90s, the company I was working for severely cut back on personnel. It felt like I was doing the job of three people, not just one. I generally ran about 3 weeks behind in returning phone calls and correspondence, so no matter what I did, I never caught up. I received anywhere from fifteen to thirty phone calls a day and every one of the callers was angry before I even said, "hello." For obvious reasons, I hated picking up the phone. The only problem was that when you don't talk to an angry person the first time they call, the level of their frustration rises exponentially.

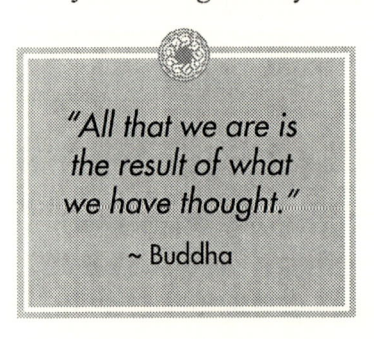

> *"All that we are is the result of what we have thought."*
> ~ Buddha

I procrastinated all the time. I hated talking to the people who called as much as they hated the information I was providing. So, I usually wrote letters in response to phone calls to avoid the callers' wrath.

One day, I went out to lunch for Chinese food with some associates. When it came time to pay the bill, we all chose a cookie and read the fortune aloud. My fortune cookie read, "You never hesitate to tackle the most difficult problems." At first I laughed. This certainly wasn't *my* cookie. But then, something inside me flashed. This *was* my fortune.

When I got back to the office I made a beeline for the copy machine. I started to copy the fortune, blowing it up bigger and bigger. I taped three sheets of paper together to make my fortune about a foot high and 3 ½ feet wide. Then, I took it back to my office and hung it up on the wall directly across from my office desk so that I would always be looking straight at it. Now my goal was clear.

It was after a month or so that I realized things had changed. I was out for lunch with a friend when she asked me, "What's wrong with you lately, you seem so relaxed. Hasn't anyone called you names or threatened you at work today?" It was then that I realized I wasn't procrastinating as much as I did before. I had been taking more phone calls when they came in and wasn't waiting so long to return the ones I missed. There were still the same number of people calling but somehow my workload felt a little lighter. Deep down inside I had made the connection; I knew that these changes must all be due to the giant fortune taped to my office wall.

My intention had been to stop procrastinating. Every time I found myself looking at the fortune cookie I was reminded, "You never hesitate to tackle the most difficult problems." Little by little I had started to adopt the behaviors I had set out to change, prompted by the constant reminder posted on my wall. It was barely something that I thought about consciously as the phone would ring. And yet, a change had indeed taken place.

Transform Your Own Life

Are you ready to allow your subconscious to help you make your love life everything you've dreamed? If you were going to change one habit or pattern that you've noticed might be holding you back from having the love you always wanted, what would it be? Would you be willing to courageously ask for what you want? Make more time for intimacy? Plan romantic nights together? Be more respectful of your own boundaries?

When you focus on what you want, you begin the process of creation. What you imagine can become your reality and often in ways you least expect.

In recent times, there have been numerous books, teachers, and scientists who convey that like attracts like throughout the universe. This theory also applies to your thoughts, feelings, and experiences. This creation thing can be easier than you think. If you want your partner to be more affectionate with you, be more affectionate yourself. Think about what you want more of in your life and focus on the positive aspect of it. If you want more romance in your life, plan a special date just for the two of you. Keep in mind that this technique works the opposite way, too. If you keep complaining to your friends that your honey never does anything nice for you, chances are, until you change your tune, your partner won't be making any changes soon.

When you focus on the positive, you will get more positive. When you focus on the negative, you will get more of that, too. How you experience your life is very much related to where you place your focus.

EXERCISE 1: Create Your Own Fortune

On the following page is your fortune cookie. Choose one habit, pattern, or belief that you would like to change and state the new behavior in a manner that will prompt your action. Remember, my fortune cookie said, "You never hesitate to tackle the most difficult problems." It did *not* say, "You are going to pick up the phone more when nasty people who pull guns on you in business meetings might be calling."

Take a few minutes to give some thought to a habit that you want to change. Before you create your fortune, make sure you are stating your desired change in a positive way.

For Example:

Instead of Writing:
You are going to stop giving in when your partner asks you to do something you don't want to do.

Write:
You always honor and respect your own boundaries.

Now you are ready to take a step toward choosing to live your life in the way that *you* desire. You are breaking the old habit as we speak and putting into play new patterns you can feel good about. Go ahead and create your new fortune now.

What does your fortune say?

The Power of Intentions

How you participate in your everyday life ultimately impacts your ability to achieve your goals and have the love life (and anything else) you truly want. Do you sit back praying that the man or woman you are interested in will ask you out for a date, or are you willing to make the first move?

Intentions are the combined focus of your personal power, creative energy, and participation in each present moment. Living your intentions can take you to your goals. The fortune cookie assignment you just did was actually an exercise in setting an intention. See, it's easier than you might think!

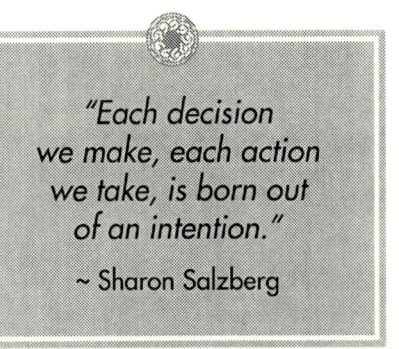

> *"Each decision we make, each action we take, is born out of an intention."*
> ~ Sharon Salzberg

Consciously setting my intentions has been part of my life for a long time. Many years ago, I was single and ready to find the next love of my life. I remember thinking that if I met someone or even saw someone that I felt attracted to that I was going to make the first move. I was not going to let my next possible partner slip through the cracks just because they might not have had the courage to approach me or didn't see the electric sparks of connection flying between us. My intention was to be fully available for love and willing to take the first step.

When I worked as a hypnotherapist, I took a few minutes before meeting with each client to prepare for our work together. As part of my pre-session ritual, I would look over any notes that I might have taken in previous visits. Then, I would state in my mind my intentions:

- I would be a clear and open channel for any information that would be of assistance to the client.

- I would be present and committed to my client's success.

- My client would find the experience to be both valuable and beneficial.

Without even realizing what I was doing, I was setting the expectation for success in both the future of my love life and the effectiveness of my client meetings.

Setting an intention is an amazing tool. In my hypnotherapy practice, my client's success rates were about 85%. In my love life, I became open to discovering true love and participating more fully in the process, and it worked! I filled my nights with dates and eventually found my someone wonderful.

I cannot guarantee that you will always get exactly what wish. However, I can promise that when you participate in your life and regularly affirm what you want, your chances of actually getting it will be increased ten-fold. What are your intentions with this life of yours?

EXERCISE 2: Stating Your Intentions

Begin by writing down your intention(s) related to your love life. Maybe you'd like to be honest with your partner about your feelings, be more open to trying something you haven't tried before, or are ready to find your soul mate. Your intention can be something you want to do for a moment, an afternoon, or the rest of your life.

To help you begin to create the changes in your life that you choose, start with something easy. Choose something that is immediately relevant for at least the next few hours or the rest of the day. Make it as simple as possible. Then, take action. Participate by making a conscious effort to manifest what you intended into your reality.

Examples:

- I will have the courage to say no to my partner's request when I recognize that I will not be honoring my own boundaries.

- I will remember to ask for help this week.

- I will be willing to consider a compromise so that we can both get more of what we want.

- From this point forward I will _____.

When you've recorded your intention, find yourself a mirror (or complete this with your partner if you are doing this process together). Look at yourself (or your partner) in the eye and speak your intention out loud. Repeat it several times. This intention can become your new reality.

SUPERCHARGE Your Intentions!

If you want to add impact to the creation of your intentions, read your statement aloud and then take some time to imagine what it would feel like to have what you are intending come to life.

Hold these feelings in your mind and body as often as you can. Experiencing the feelings will add impact to how quickly you manifest what you want.

For Couples

Setting intentions together can be a great way to connect during good times and challenging ones. Start each morning with a 2-minute exercise of exchanging your intentions for the day. This can be an wonderful opportunity to support your partner and your relationship as you both bring what you wish to your lives.

Letting Go of Limiting Beliefs Meditation: 12 minutes

Begin by closing your eyes. Take a deep breath in, and hold it. Exhaling very slowly, just relaxing and letting go of any tension, any tightness you might be holding in your body or your mind. And, another deep breath in, holding it as long as you comfortably can. And now, exhaling slowly and gently, becoming more and more relaxed with each breath. Just slowing down, and letting

CONTINUED ▶

go. Breathing easily and gently, going deeper and deeper into a peaceful state of relaxation.

PAUSE 3 SECONDS...

And you know that you are perfectly safe here at this time. And no one and nothing can harm you. So you can just take your time to relax, let go, and unwind.

And you may begin to notice that your eyes are becoming comfortably closed. And your eyelids are starting to feel heavy. Heavy and so relaxed, calm and peaceful.

And a feeling of relaxation flows to your head and your face, as all the muscles in your head and face relax. Any tension or tightness is just beginning to melt away. You feel calm and peaceful, just like you do when you are about to drift off to sleep.

And now that gentle flow of relaxation moves into your shoulders and through your chest, as all the muscles of your shoulders and chest area relax. And that warm peaceful feeling flows down your arms and your back to the base of your spine, continuing down your legs all the way to the tips of your toes. Your mind is at ease and your entire body feels heavy, heavy and perfectly relaxed.

PAUSE 5 SECONDS...

Now imagine that you are lying down in the most comfortable and relaxing place. Whatever comes to mind is perfect, just so long as you feel comfortable.

And as you look around you notice that a masseuse has joined you. And there is something very warm and loving about their presence. They tell you that they have come today to give you a relaxing massage that will help you transform any limiting thoughts, beliefs, or feelings of what you cannot do, be, or have.

CONTINUED ▶

Your massage begins and the masseuse intuitively knows how to reach any place in your body that might be tense or tight. And as their hands move from your shoulders to your lower back, any emotion or limiting belief that had been trapped in your body is magically released. As your massage continues, you can easily and gently let go of anything that might be holding you back from experiencing the life you want. So just take a moment to feel how wonderful it is to experience this transformational massage.

PAUSE 10 SECONDS . . .

Good. Now your masseuse lets you know that during this massage, your mind, body, and spirit are re-awakening completely to the divine plan, the truth: You can have anything you desire.

And to show you how you can attract to you anything you want, your masseuse asks you to think of something you would really like to have in your life. It can be to find a new job you enjoy, to meet the love of your life, or to learn how to communicate more effectively. Whatever it is that would make your life more enjoyable for you, just bring it to your mind's eye now.

PAUSE 3 SECONDS . . .

Now imagine that you already have what it is that you thought of. Begin to see yourself with this new addition in your life. How has your life changed? Are you happier? More content? Excited or more peaceful? Just focus on the feelings that you are experiencing now that you have what it is that you've wished for.

PAUSE 10 SECONDS . . .

Good. Now that you have created the perfect version of what you want in your life, experience the feeling of gratitude. Are you saying in your mind "I'm lucky"? "I'm so happy now"? Whatever you feel, just hold these feelings in your heart, your mind, and your

CONTINUED ▶

> entire body. Feel how thankful you are for finally experiencing everything that you wanted.
>
> **PAUSE 10 SECONDS...**
>
> Good. Your masseuse reminds you that you have reawakened a part of yourself that knows what it feels like to be connected to all that is, and the power of co-creation with the universe. You can use this technique anytime to bring into your life anything that you desire. From this point forward, there is nothing that can stop you from creating and experiencing the best version of life you can imagine.
>
> Now notice now how confident and excited you feel about this reawakened aspect of yourself. And take a moment to thank your masseuse for what you have experienced today, and when you are ready, say goodbye for now.
>
> **PAUSE 5 SECONDS...**
>
> And now as I count from three to one you will become more awake, more alert, and ready to live your life fully. Confident and filled with love.
>
> 3 ... feeling full of natural vibrant energy,
> 2 ... filled with joy and happiness, and
> 1 ... eyes wide open, feeling good and ready to enjoy the rest of your day.

Your Words Create Your Reality

Many years ago I heard a story from a friend about her client, Maureen. Being a very positive thinker, Maureen subscribed to the premise that she could, in fact, create anything in her life that she wanted.

Maureen grew up very poor and had to work hard to get the things in her life that she felt would make her happy. She had a job that paid her well and a condo in the best part of town. She was engaged to someone who she thought was her prince charming come to life. Now all she wanted was a Mercedes. Not any Mercedes, but a two-seater convertible known as a 560SL.

Maureen was dead set on getting this car. She started by setting her intention and then writing it down. "I'm going to get a Mercedes 560 SL, whatever it takes." Then someone told her that if you write your intention more often, there would be a better chance of getting what she wanted sooner. There really wasn't anything wrong with her Honda Accord, it was already paid off and only 2-years-old, but Maureen really wanted the Mercedes. At the time, she just didn't have the money to buy it. So off she went, writing her new affirmation daily.

For the first few weeks Maureen wrote, "I'm going to get a Mercedes 560SL, whatever it takes," about fifty times a day. Next, she heard that speaking her dream aloud might even increase that chances of achieving her goals that much faster. So, she began telling everyone she met, "I'm going to get a Mercedes 560SL, whatever it takes." Maureen began to sound like a broken record. During that month, there wasn't anyone who came in contact with Maureen who wasn't 100% sure that she was going to get that darn car.

Several months later, I learned that Maureen was in the hospital. She had a broken collar bone, fractured skull, broken nose, broken leg, and more than 200 stitches. Maureen had been driving home from work and her car was hit by another car whose driver didn't see that the traffic in front of him had stopped. He hit Maureen's Accord and then she smashed into the car in front of her. The doctors said that it was a miracle that she lived.

Maureen was in the hospital for 41 days and endured several surgeries to correct the problems that she encountered. The doctors told her that she may always walk with a bit of a limp but that eventually the scars on her face would fade.

If you haven't already guessed the ending of the story, the following month, Maureen received a settlement check from the insurance company. After her medical expenses were paid, her compensation for her totaled Accord and her pain and suffering was about a hundred dollars more than the amount of money she needed to buy her dream car, the midnight blue 1989 mint condition Mercedes 560SL that she was intent on getting, no matter what it takes.

Although Maureen was severely injured, this was really a success story. She set out to get something that she wanted and she achieved it, albeit probably not in the most graceful way possible. This is a good reminder that the words you use to ask for what you want are just as important as asking in the first place. Maureen was intent on getting her Mercedes, "whatever it takes."

To ensure you are attracting what you really want, always state things in the positive. Instead of saying, "I want to get out of debt," say, "I want to live a financially secure life," or, "I am thankful for total financial freedom."

When I set an intention, I usually begin by stating or outlining what I want and then I ask for that "or something better." Next, I state that I would like the object of my desires to come to me gracefully and easily and in alignment with the highest good for all involved. Remember, you can decide how your intentions or desires manifest.

> ### Ask for What You Want or Something Better
>
> As you begin to create your dream life and start asking for what you want, be willing to consider that you might not be aware of everything that could be available to you.
>
> Make sure you:
>
> - Think clearly about what you are asking for.
> - State it in the positive.
> - Ask for what you want, "or something better."

Take Your Intentions to the World

There are several ways in which you can participate in bringing your goals, dreams, and intentions to life. Whether you want to be a part of a romantic relationship that grows more loving every day, lose twenty pounds, get a job that you love, or like Maureen, even create your very own dream car, taking an active role will expedite the process.

Once you know what you want, write it down, say it out loud, and imagine what it feels like to have it. Hold within you the feeling of gratitude for receiving what you've requested as if it has already happened. Be willing to tell everyone you can about what it is you want to have in your life. Sometimes connecting with just the right person will help you realize your dream.

Connecting to What You Want

It is theorized that there are only six degrees of separation between every person on the planet. This means that someone I know, knows someone else, who knows someone else, who knows someone else and the fifth someone else will know the person I am trying to meet. This idea was originally proposed by Hungarian writer Frigyes Karinthy in a short story called *Chains* in 1929 and subsequently was put to the test by several people between 1950 and 2001.

While everything I want may be as close as one degree away, I just don't know who or which direction that one degree might be. I am certain that if I wanted to find a publisher for my next book and I literally asked everyone that I came in contact with for an entire week if they could help (this means the server at lunch out with friends, the man in front of me in line at the bank, the person jogging next to me on the treadmill at the gym, and so forth), someone *will* either be a publisher, a published writer or editor, or know someone who is.

> *"Be careful what you set your heart on, for it will surely be yours."*
> ~ Ralph Waldo Emerson

This method has worked for me a number of times. I found a new dentist that I loved through a conversation with my attorney. I found a buyer for my car by talking to an insurance agent whose brother was looking for a vehicle. Along the way I've learned about numerous good restaurants, leads for new business, and countless other hot tips from people who were not friends, and some of whom were even perfect strangers.

Miracle Networking

While hanging out with a friend one night who insisted that she could no longer be trusted to find her own dates (after several recent disasters), we came up with an idea I was certain would help. I explained my belief that her next boyfriend could really be as close as one or two degrees of separation away from her. The only challenge was that we just didn't know whom to ask in order for her to meet him.

After several attempts to convince her that she could start asking virtual strangers to help her find her next boyfriend, we came up with another plan. We would bring together eight acquaintances and ask everyone to bring a friend. To make it more fun, we made it a potluck dinner and told everyone it was an evening of Miracle Networking. We asked that they come to the party hoping to add something to their lives, from a new job to a used bicycle, or anything else they desired.

Since that first night, I have been hosting Miracle Networking groups on and off for more than 15 years purely for my own enjoyment. Even with gatherings of just ten people it seems that there are always matches made, if not that day, then within the 30 days that follow. I have found that the mere action of speaking your desire aloud helps draw whatever you want to you. The Miracle Networking groups are a fun way to meet new people and help everyone attract more of what they want into their lives.

If you are working this book on your own, you can use the format on the next page to create your own gathering. If you are part of a Circle, you will find out how magical this process can be this week. Don't forget to bring a friend to your *More Love, More Joy!* Circle.

Make Your Weekly Commitments

Choose a step from your Action List (from Chapter 2) that you will complete this week to make progress toward your relationship goals. Also, spend some time doing "something wonderful" just for you.

Tip of the Week:
Ask for what you want, "or something better!"

Miracle Networking Gathering

What You'll Need to Get Started:

- **Name Tags**
- **Paper**
  (for each person to take notes)
- **A Timer or Watch**
  (with a digital read out)
- **Pens**
- **Friends**
  (Have Circle Members bring one friend or acquaintance to the meeting so the group is between 12-25 people total.)

You'll also need three volunteers, each with a specific job:

- **Greeter:**
  Gives everyone a name tag and supplies for taking notes.

- **Moderator/Time Keeper:**
  Monitors mingle time, calls the group to a circle (to begin networking). Keeps sharing time to 2-3 minutes per person and lets everyone know when the gathering has come to an end.

- **Secretary:**
  Writes each person's name, phone number or e-mail address, and the one to three things that they wish to network for or add to their lives. The Secretary also records everyone's progress, matches, and successes during the 30 days following the gathering (regardless of if the successes were as a direct result of the gathering). At the end of the 30 days, the Secretary e-mails a progress report to all the participants.

How it Works:

Ideally you'll want to have between 12-25 people. Everyone including the Moderator, Secretary, and Greeter participate in sharing. Make sure the Secretary provides his or her contact information so that everyone can notify him or her of any connections they make with their desired goals in the following month.

1. When the Moderator calls the group together and everyone gathers into a circle with their pens and paper, each person will have 2-3 minutes to share the following:

A. Name
   B. Phone number or e-mail address
   C. The one to three things they would like to add to their lives (ie. a used bicycle, to join a book group, find a new dentist, or to meet the love of their life).

   The Moderator will watch the time and use a raised hand to let people when to wrap things up.

2. Everyone in the circle takes notes, writing down names, numbers, and wishes. If anyone has what the person speaking is looking for or can provide a lead, then they can share it with the speaker *after* everyone in the circle has taken their turn.

3. Once everyone has had a chance to speak, the Moderator will ask if anyone knows of a match or lead for what anyone has expressed interest in. Connections can be made at this time.

4. Before the group ends, the Moderator can remind everyone to keep their lists (of other people's requests) handy for the next 30 days. If participants come in contact with a match for someone, they can contact the person directly.

5. At the end of the 30 days, the Secretary will then e-mail all participants to let everyone know what connections or successes others have experienced as a result of the group.

Note: Many times people get what they are hoping for within the 30 days immediately following the gathering. However, sometimes the connections or solutions don't always come directly though one of the participants. Regardless, any success is worth celebrating!

You have now learned (or have been reminded) that there are many ways to begin setting your desires into motion. You can truly participate in the creation of your life and everything in it, from your next true love or ideal job to your dream home or financial independence.

So, don't be afraid to let a fortune cookie change your life. Set an intention for today or for as long as you wish. Let like attract like. Ask for what you want and be willing to tell the world about it. Every one of these actions will help you attract anything you want.

FOR CIRCLE MEMBERS

Week 7 Homework:
Complete prior to attending your 7th Circle
- Read Chapter 8
- Start Exercise 1: Do as much or as little as you'd like
- Complete your weekly commitments

Bring to the Meeting:
- Your *More Love, More Joy!* book
- A new journal or special paper to create your Wishbook. (This should be separate from the journal you've been using for your other homework.)
- Any art supplies you want for personalizing your Wishbook

In Your Circle You Will:
- Continue working on Exercise 1
- Do Exercise 2

8

Discovering Your Desires & Building Your Wishbook

"Where there is great love, there are always wishes."
~ Willa Cather

In this chapter, you'll be identifying and recording the beginnings of your own unique Wishbook. This is the a journal of what you desire at various times throughout your life. It can be a really fun way for you to rediscover yourself and see how your love life can grow and improve.

Before beginning your Wishbook, remember that this can be an opportunity to recreate yourself. This is your chance to start new, to step boldly into your true self. It's your turn to be authentic and confidently request what would make you happy either within your existing relationship or from a future partner.

When you begin, you can either write your answers here in this book or use your own special journal. Write with a favorite pen, colored markers, paste in pictures, or do whatever you feel is right to personalize your Wishbook. You can be as creative as you like.

As you start to answer these questions, be honest with yourself and true to what your heart desires, regardless of whether or not you think receiving it is possible. Although discovering and asking for what you truly want may be something new for you, remember that deep down inside you are worthy. You deserve to be happy, to be treated with kindness, and to be loved in exactly the way you wish. Keep in mind that just identifying your wishes and desires can be the first step to manifesting the kind of love you want in your life. Writing it down and speaking the words aloud take you one step even closer to your new reality.

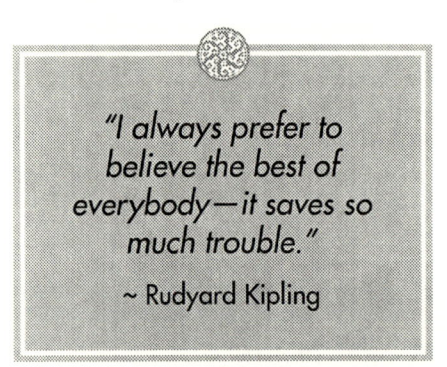

> *"I always prefer to believe the best of everybody—it saves so much trouble."*
>
> ~ Rudyard Kipling

Lastly, since as individuals we are always changing, we suggest you review your answers annually, when you are between relationships, or as often as you like. Keep in mind that if what you wrote no longer feels like exactly what you'd wish for anymore, you can change your answers at any time.

Are You in a Relationship Now?

If so, try to answer each question honestly without concern for what you believe your partner may or may not agree to do. Don't hold back. This is your opportunity to participate in the future of your (collective) relationship. The focus here is on recognizing what *you* wish for in your love life, without any limitations. Be courageous enough to ask for what you really want, it just might change your life.

For Everyone

Regardless of whether or not you are in relationship now, the questions and map in this chapter can give you the opportunity to begin anew. This is a chance to put the past behind you and put into play your ideal version of your love life, starting today.

When you have completed the work in this chapter, we invite you to use your Wishbook as a tool to initiate a dialog with your partner. This can be a chance for both of you to enjoy a more evolved relationship and can help you get more of what you've identified you'd like from one another.

Make Your Weekly Commitments

Choose a step from your Action List (from Chapter 2) that you will complete this week to make progress toward your relationship goals. Also, spend some time doing "something wonderful" just for you.

> **Tip of the Week:**
> We are always growing and evolving. This week, how can you honor and appreciate who you are today?

EXERCISE 1: Make Your Personal Wishbook

Please take as much time as you like with the questions on the following pages. You can answer one question a day before bed or dive right and finish them all in a night. Whatever your pace, make it just right for you. As you look through the list, you can focus on the questions that appeal to you. Leave out the ones that aren't quite your style and make up your own questions if you find that we didn't include something you feel might be important to share.

If you stumble upon a question and your immediate answer is, "I don't know," you have most likely come upon something of personal value. Do your best to push forward. Dig deep and answer the question even if it feels a little challenging. You can always change your mind later if your first response doesn't turn out to be quite right for you.

You may want to use a new journal specifically for this exercise. Be as creative as you want and provide as much insight and information as you can. Your Wishbook will allow you to share with a partner what you love and how to best take care of you. The more detailed you can be, the better. Tuck in to-go menus, business cards, flyers, and print-outs of web pages. Add any visuals that would help your partner better understand what you're requesting.

If what you would really like is a day at the spa or tickets to a ball game as one of your "do something nice for me" requests, see if you can pick up a spa menu or game schedule that includes where to buy tickets. That way, there won't be any question about what you'd like or how to get it. This can actually help your partner know that whatever they give you will be perfect.

You may find that some of the questions can inspire multiple answers. Include as much of what you can think of now, as you can always add more later. The more detailed and specific you can be about what you want, the easier it will be for someone to grant your wish.

When you are done, if you find there is additional information that you would like to share with your partner, feel free to add anything else that might be helpful for him or her to know. Remember to keep your requests on a positive note. Take your time and have fun!

My Wishbook

BIRTHDAYS

1. Describe your perfect birthday celebration.

   _____
   _____
   _____
   _____
   _____
   _____
   _____
   _____

2. What wouldn't you want to do on your birthday?

   _____
   _____
   _____
   _____

3. Is it important that your partner remembers your birthday and plans something special?

   ❏ Yes   ❏ No   Month/Day/Year_____

4. What kind of birthday gift(s) would you generally like to receive from your partner? Do you have any specific desires for this year?

5. Is there a special food, place, or tradition that you want on your birthday? If so, describe it.

6. What would you like your partner to do or say to let you know that you are loved and appreciated on your birthday?

7. If your partner wanted to surprise you on your birthday, here are 3-4 ideas of events you would enjoy.

___

8. Who would you want to include in your birthday celebration?

___

9. Is it okay for everyone else to know your age?

❑ Yes   ❑ No

ANNIVERSARIES

10. What anniversaries would you like to celebrate? Write the date after any you select.

    ❑ Wedding _____

    ❑ First Date _____

    ❑ Day You Met _____

    ❑ Date You Moved In Together _____

    ❑ Day of Your First Sexual Encounter _____

    ❑ Other _____

11. Is it important to you that your partner knows how long you've been together and the date of your anniversary?

    ❑ Yes   ❑ No

12. Describe your ideal anniversary celebration.

    _____
    _____
    _____
    _____
    _____
    _____
    _____
    _____
    _____
    _____

13. What wouldn't you want to do on your anniversary?

14. How important is it for your partner to remember and plan something special?

15. What kind of gift(s) would you generally like to receive from your partner for your anniversary? Do you have any specific requests for this year?

16. What would you like your partner to do or say to let you know that you are loved and appreciated on your anniversary?

17. What would the best anniversary surprise be? List 3-4 ideas of anniversary surprises you would enjoy.

SPECIAL REQUESTS

18. After a difficult day, what I really need and want is . . .

_____
_____
_____
_____
_____

19. If my partner really wanted to do something special for me, here are some ideas for things I would enjoy.

_____
_____
_____
_____
_____
_____

20. In challenging times, I want my partner to say . . .

_____
_____

and do . . .

_____
_____

21. I have a hard time asking for . . .

22. It would be easier for me to consider a compromise if my partner . . .

23. I need my partner's understanding when . . .

Or with . . .

24. I just want to be held (or _____)
    and told it's okay when . . .

25. I could use my partner's help solving my problems when . . .

26. I appreciate when my partner handles . . .

27. It's difficult for me to feel like my life in balance when my partner . . .

___

28. When I need help with _____,
    the best way to support me would be . . .

___

COMMUNICATION

29. I'm a better listener when my partner . . .

___

30. I know my partner is listening to me when . . .

31. I'd prefer to talk with my partner about the following in private:

32. I'd prefer my partner didn't tell anyone else about . . .

EMOTIONS

33. When I'm angry, I really need . . .

34. When I'm frustrated, I want . . .

35. If something happens and I feel sad, I wish my partner would . . .

36. Here are some things that always help me feel good . . .

37. I need my partner's patience with . . .

38. I feel embarrassed when my partner . . .

LOVE & ROMANCE

39. A few ideas for the perfect romantic date with me would be . . .

40. My favorite restaurants are . . .

_____
_____
_____
_____
_____

41. I like to hear my partner say, "I love you," _____ times per
    (circle one)   day   week   month

42. My partner could show me I am respected by . . .

_____
_____
_____
_____
_____

43. My partner could show me I am loved by . . .

_____
_____
_____
_____
_____
_____
_____

44. My partner could show me I am appreciated by . . .

45. My partner could show me I am attractive by . . .

SEX

46. Describe your ideal setting for intimacy. Candles? Dimmed lights? Romantic locations?

47. I feel most comfortable having sexual intimacy when my partner . . .

48. What would your ideal lover do or say?

49. How important for you to hear "I love you" during or after sex?

50. In what non-verbal ways do you (or could you) signal your partner that you are in the mood?

51. When is it easiest for you to have a conversation about sex?

52. Is there anything you feel uncomfortable talking about? Can your partner do or say anything to help you feel more comfortable?

53. How important is foreplay to you?

54. What would you like as a warmer upper to help put you in the mood?

55. Are there some things that you don't want to participate in sexually? If so, what?

160 More Love, More Joy!

EXERCISE 2: Create Your Body Pleasure Map

Using the outlines provided, create a map to illustrate what brings you pleasure and where your boundaries lie. Make up your own key for what you might enjoy, using whatever symbols you designate. Little swirls can mean light kissing, stars might mean caressing, deep massaging, or whatever would bring you pleasure. Little x's might mean "do not enter." The more creative and descriptive you can be the better. Here is a sample to give you some more ideas:

| THE KEY TO MY PLEASURE ||
SYMBOL	MEANING
@	kisses
~~	massage
▨	no tickling zone
)(	pinching
⊓⊓	biting
∞	sucking
-++-	pet lightly
⊗	do not enter

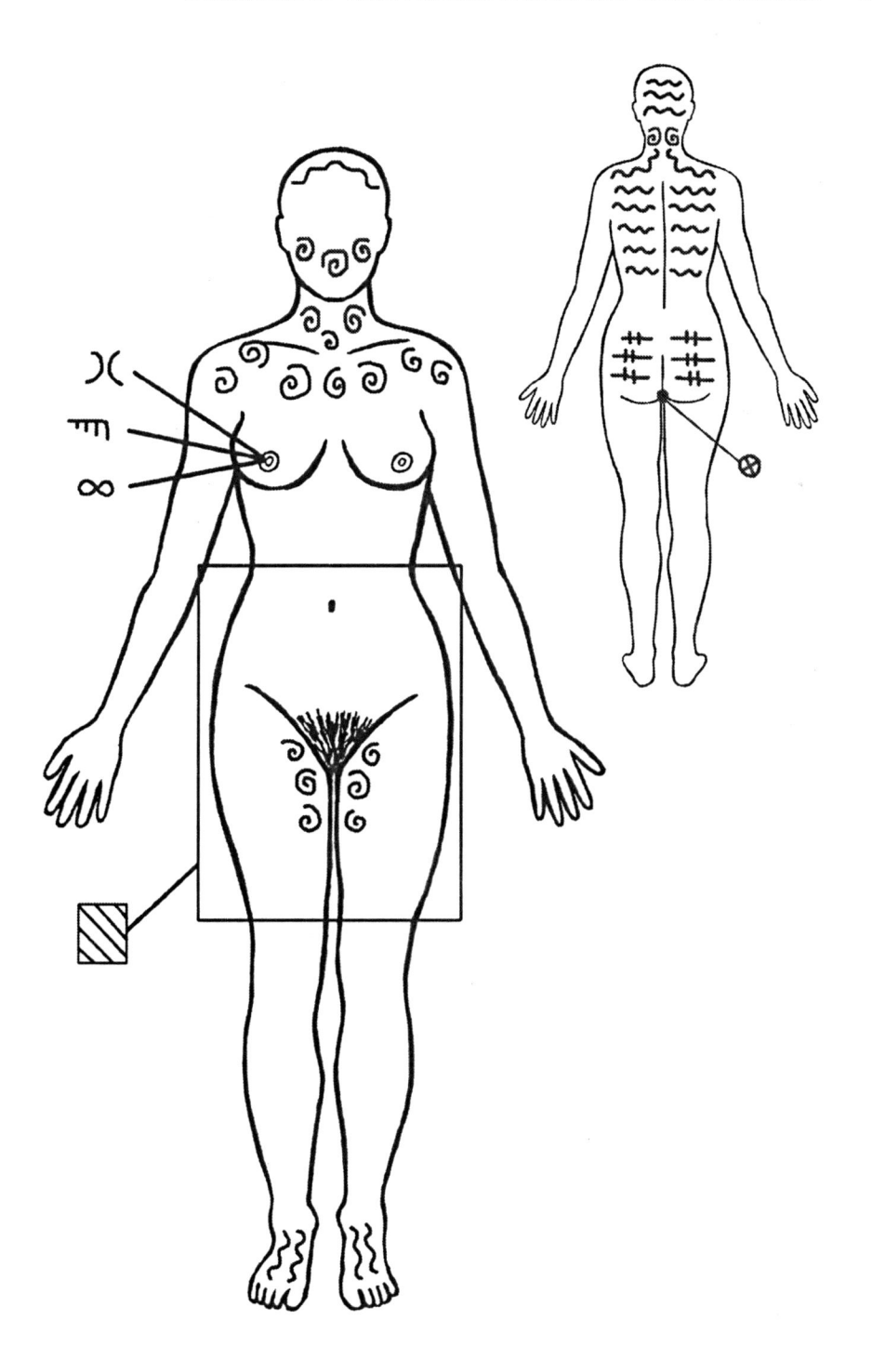

Discovering Your Desires & Building Your Wishbook 161

THE KEY TO MY PLEASURE

SYMBOL	MEANING

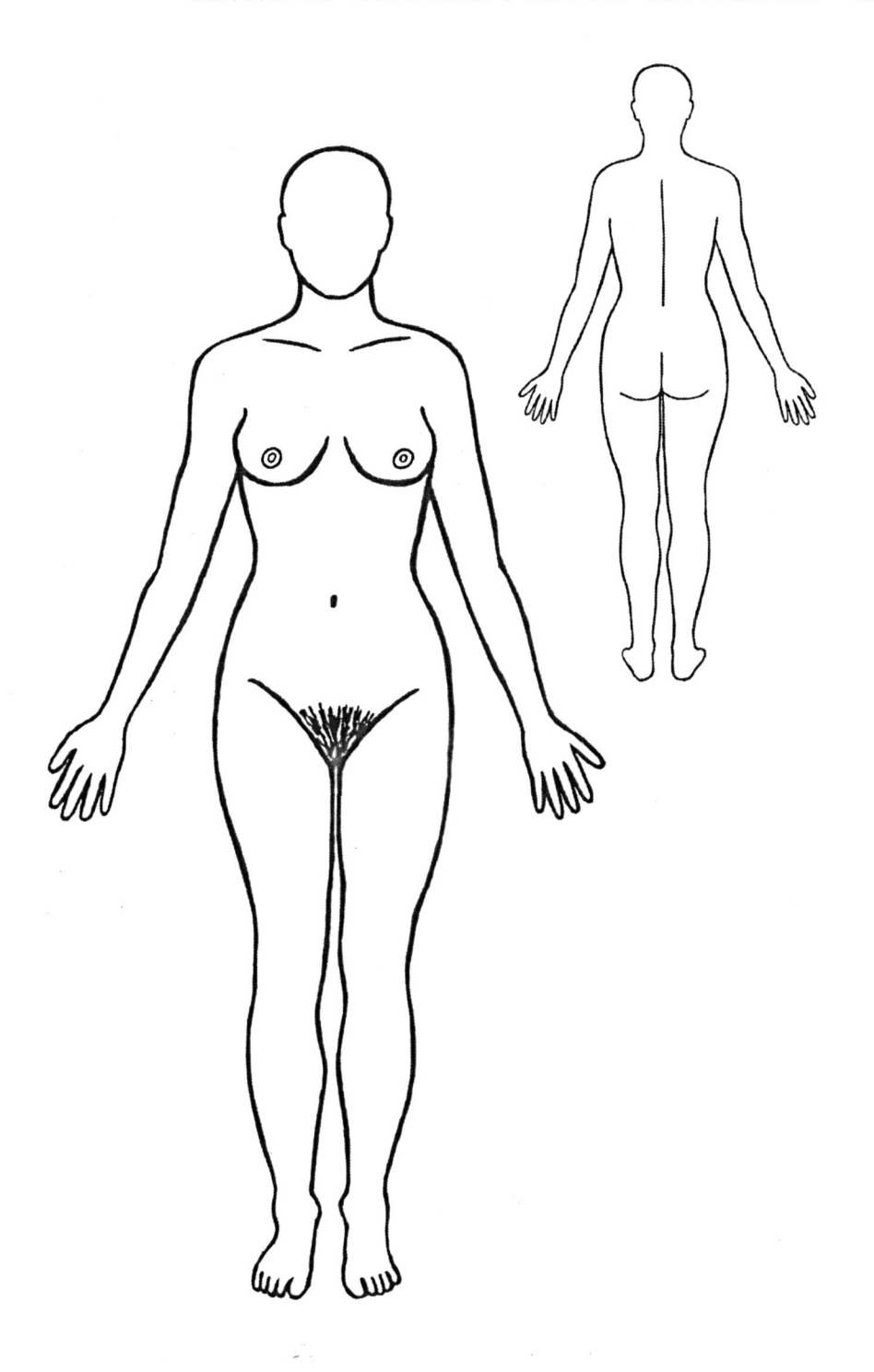

DISCOVERING YOUR DESIRES & BUILDING YOUR WISHBOOK   163

THE KEY TO MY PLEASURE	
SYMBOL	MEANING

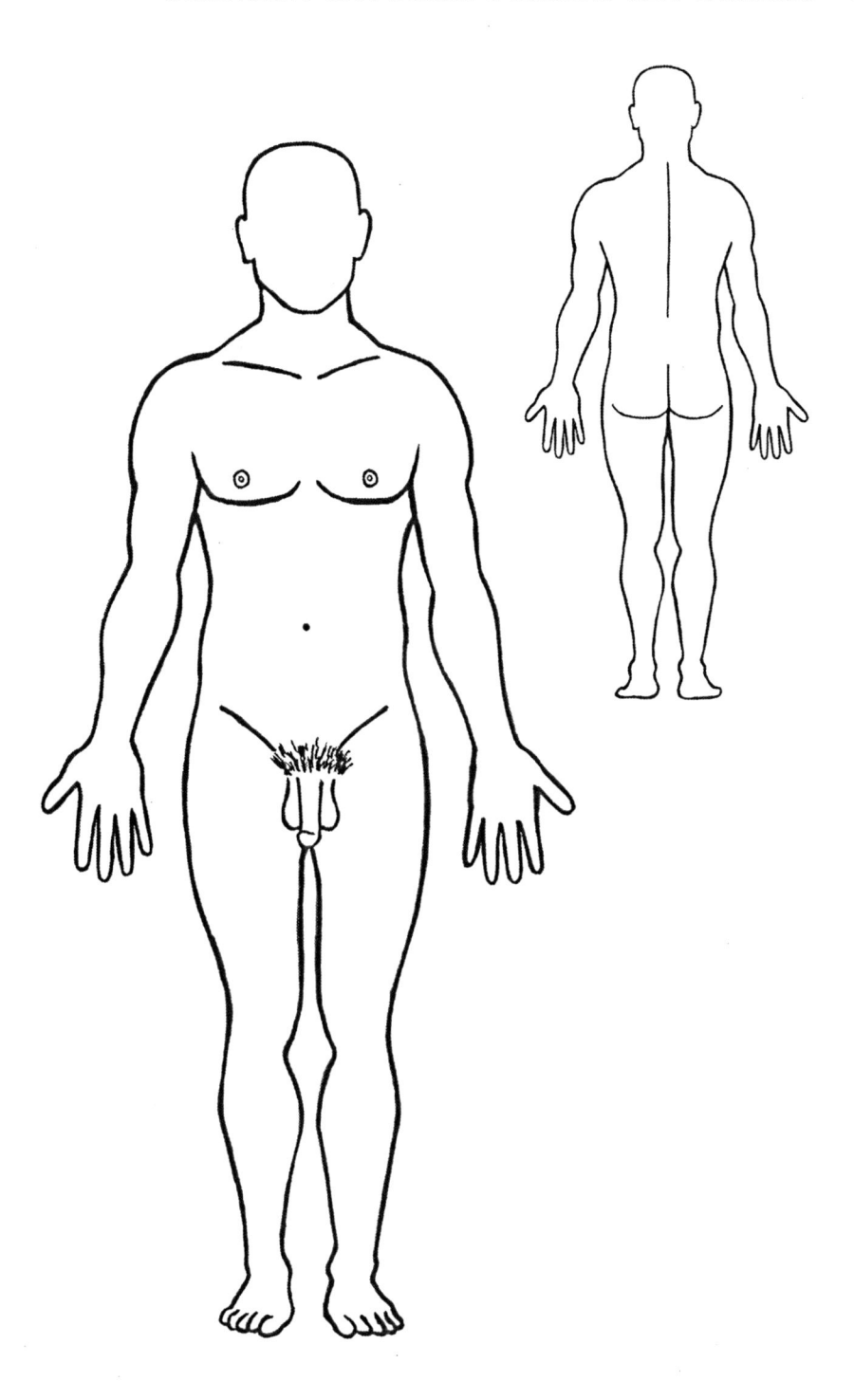

Discovering Your Desires & Building Your Wishbook 165

FOR CIRCLE MEMBERS

Week 8 Homework:
Complete prior to attending your 8th Circle
- Read Chapter 9
- Continue working on your Wishbook
- Complete your weekly commitments

Bring to the Meeting:
- Your *More Love, More Joy!* book
- A journal/notebook and a pen/pencil

In Your Circle You Will Complete:
- Exercises 1-4

9

Asking for What You Want

"You've got to ask! Asking is, in my opinion, the world's most powerful—and neglected—secret to success and happiness."

~ Percy Ross

Look at how far you've come! If you haven't done something wonderful for yourself this week, get out your calendar and make a date to celebrate your success. This is a great time to honor yourself for the commitments you have made to caring for yourself in a loving way, letting go of anything holding you back, boldly (or not so boldly) stepping into your power, and remembering or discovering what will bring more joy and pleasure to your love life.

EXERCISE 1: Identifying Your Growth

Take a few minutes to reflect on what you learned so far and see if you relate to any of the following sentences. How have you or your beliefs or perceptions changed since you started this process?

- ❏ I believe in myself more now.
- ❏ I know I always have choices to create changes in my life.
- ❏ Only I can decide to make myself happy. I am ultimately responsible for my emotions and my state of being.
- ❏ I feel excited about the possibilities in my love relationship.

❏ I am more comfortable communicating with people in many areas of my life.

❏ I can see that loving and caring for myself is essential to experiencing the most complete relationships possible.

❏ I feel lighter and less weighed down by the past.

❏ I can easily think of many ways to bring more joy and happiness to my life.

❏ I am more confident in my relationship with my partner.

❏ I know more about myself now and have gained clarity about what I want at this time in my life.

❏ I know my next relationship can be better than any I've had before.

❏ I've realized that only I can decide who I am or what I want to do in my life.

❏ I recognize the value of both giving and receiving.

❏ I know that if my partner and I both ask for what we want in our relationship, it will help us create more a more balanced and fulfilling life together.

❏ Asking for what I want feels much easier than it was before.

Have you noticed that anything else has changed in your life for the better since you've begun this process?

Asking for What You Want

Now that you have created your Wishbook, it's time to learn how to put it to use. This week, we'll focus on preparing to share your Wishbook, learning how to ask for your wishes, and finally, introducing your Wishbook to your partner.

COMMUNICATION TIPS

💡 Before an Important Conversation

Send 'Em Love

Just prior to your conversation, take a few minutes to think about the person you'll be speaking with and send them love. Not necessarily romantic love (at least if that wouldn't be appropriate), but the kind of universal love you might feel for a newborn child or your best friend. Regardless of how unnatural or unusual this might seem to you, I assure you that no matter who you are speaking with, this technique works.

So, close your eyes, quiet your mind, and connect to the feeling of love within your heart. Focus on sending that feeling of love from your heart to the person you'll be speaking with, and if you are open to it, say in your mind, "I love you." No matter what the nature of your conversation, this gesture will help you create the best possible outcome for all.

Imagine the Best Possible Outcome

Here is another valuable pre-communication tool. Begin by considering what the best-case scenario might be for yourself and anyone else the situation involves. Then, close your eyes and imagine how you'd like your conversation to play out. See in your mind everything that will happen, every detail of how the ideal outcome is created.

After you've finished the scene, take some time to experience what it would feel like to have everything you've envisioned. Hold these feelings in your mind and body for as long as you can. Finally, focus on your feeling of gratitude for how perfectly this situation transpired, as if it has already happened.

💡 Asking for Your Wishes Using the "I Love You" Sandwich

By far the best and most effective tool I've learned to help me get more of what I want is something that I call the "I Love You" Sandwich. I guarantee, when used as directed, this process will help you get more of what you want, more often, not just in your love relationships but in any area of your life.

When you want a conversation to have a successful outcome, you may recall that the key is to keep your audience listening. Maintaining someone's attention can sometimes be a challenge when you have something difficult or uncomfortable for them to hear. Using the "I Love You" Sandwich helps your listener remain receptive (rather than defensive), allowing them to hear your requests clearly.

The "I Love You" Sandwich in Action

Step 1: The First Slice of Bread

Begin by saying something that lets the other person know that you value the relationship you have and that you care about them. Use a statement in which you are supportive and loving if possible. Say something both honest and nice which will perk their interest in what you are saying. Note: You do not need to use the words, "I love you," if this is not appropriate. A compliment will work just fine.

Example:

"Jim, I want you to know that I love you and I appreciate all your dedication to our relationship."

Step 2: The Meat

This thought includes the important piece of information you want to share.

Example:

"This is why it is difficult for me to tell you that I simply cannot tolerate your cigar smoking in the house anymore. Either the cigars go or I do."

Step 3: The Second Slice of Bread

This second piece of "I love you" bread helps keep the listener on board and reminds them that you are invested in the future of your relationship together. Again, it isn't necessary to say the words, "I love you." Just deliver a compliment or another appropriate, kind message.

Example:

> "It is important that you know I truly love and appreciate you. I hope that you will agree to respect my wishes, because I want us to be together for a very long time."

You may find that you feel more comfortable adding a little slice of cheese, tomato, or some mustard in the middle to better explain yourself. Just remember to start and end with something stated in the positive. Tailor what you say to the type of relationship you have together. You may want to tell the other person that you respect, value, or admire them, or that you value the relationship you share. Most importantly, be genuine. The way you speak to your gardener should be very different from how you communicate with your mother.

EXERCISE 2: Practice Using the "I Love You" Sandwich

Now that you've seen how the "I Love You" Sandwich works, practice asking in your own words for what you want. Find a partner and take turns role playing or just practice out loud on your own.

Example Scenario:

> Your mother said something that hurt your feelings the last time you spoke. You want to be honest with her because you don't want her to say something like this again. What do you tell her?

Here is a possible response:

Step 1: "Mom, I really appreciate how much our relationship has grown over the last few years."

Step 2: "Which is why I want to let you know that when you said that I would never find a man if I didn't stop working so many hours, I really felt hurt."

Step 3: "It would be helpful for me if in the future you were more sensitive to my feelings because I love you and I want the future of our relationship to continue to get better and better."

Now you respond to these scenes (or choose a scenario from your own life) and practice using the "I Love You" Sandwich.

1. Your partner has been spending a lot of extra nights at work in the last 6 months and as much as you trust them, you are feeling neglected. Tell them how you feel and what your needs are.

2. It seems your partner is conveniently unavailable whenever the kids need attention and care. You are feeling as though you are doing all the work. Tell them that what you want is a partnership with shared parenting responsibilities.

3. Your fiancé has (in your opinion) a terrible shopping habit. You are concerned that when you are married they will spend all the money you both earn. You'd rather be saving the money you have together for an early retirement. Tell them about your concerns.

4. Your best friend is unhappy that you have gotten back together with your ex, who your friend thinks wasn't very good to you. Let her know that you would appreciate her support and you don't want to lose her friendship.

5. Your son has been hanging around with kids you don't trust and you are worried that he might get in trouble. Tell him honestly how you feel, ask him for what you want, and explain why.

6. Your gardener has been showing up inconsistently to maintain your yard, even though you've been paying him regularly. He does a good job otherwise and you want to maintain the relationship. Let him know that you'd like him to come every week as you both agreed.

MORE COMMUNICATION TIPS

💬 Introducing Your Wishbook to Your Partner

For Couples Working Together

If you were lucky enough to work on the book together, great! Take time to plan a special date to honor the work you've done together.

When you are ready, you can take turns sharing your Wishbook one at a time or just exchange books. Open your hearts and be willing to stretch. Honor your own boundaries. Be open to saying yes to things you never thought were interesting before and say no when something just isn't right for you. Trust your hearts, be courageous, and most of all, have fun. Remember to revisit your individual Wishbooks as often as you like and share with your partner any changes you make.

For Individuals

Now that you have answered your Wishbook questions and determined what you'd like from your partner, the next step is asking them to help you. Another option would be to use the "I Love You" Sandwich technique you just learned. Throughout this book we have shared many communication tips and tools to help you get more of what you want. So, at this point, asking may be the easy part.

> **What to do:** Give this conversation the attention it deserves. Find a time to talk when you won't be disturbed and make sure you have your partner's undivided attention. Bring your Wishbook and Body Map that you created in Chapter 8. Don't forget that your partner may be excited to learn what you have to share. Speak slowly and clearly. Allow yourself to be surprised by your partner's response. Be open and curious to hear more about what your partner would like, too. Stay committed to creating a more mutually enjoyable relationship while honoring your own desires and boundaries.
>
> **What not to do:** Talking while the television is on or while one of you is working may not be the most effective time to communicate. Also, try not to initiate the conversation about this work in bed, unless you just want to share your Body Map, which may lend itself

nicely to that location. Don't whine, raise your voice, or become argumentative. Don't assume you aren't going to get what you want. Don't give up before you start.

Sample Script: "Honey, I love you and I want to help our love continue to grow and feel more exciting for both of us. I've been journaling about what would help me feel like our relationship was more fulfilling and I'd like to share it with you." (This is when you'd present your Wishbook.) "I'm also very interested in learning more about what you would like, too. Maybe I could do something differently that you'd enjoy more. Is that something that would be of interest to you?"

[TIP] If Your Wishbook Talk Needs a Little Extra Boost...WIIFM!

Whether you are introducing your Wishbook or having any conversation about something important, you can always impact the end result by considering your requests from the other person's perspective. WIIFM stands for What's In It For Me?

When you get ready to talk with your partner about your Wishbook, don't forget to let them know what's in it for them; this will peak their interest and help keep them on-board. If you'd like your partner to participate in creating their own Wishbook, try using one of the following WIIFM based statements:

- "I would love it if you were open to creating your own Wishbook, too. If you did, you could probably get your needs met better because I would finally understand what you would like and I wouldn't have to worry about being wrong."

- "If you created your own Wishbook and Body Pleasure Map, I would have a better idea of how to please you, and then maybe you could get more of what you want in bed."

- "Your Wishbook could help you get more of what you want from me and we could have an even happier, more balanced, and fulfilling relationship together."

Hopefully, if you use one of these suggestions you'll have them hooked. Who wouldn't want to get more of what they want and have a partner who is interested in helping them get it?

EXERCISE 3: Sharing Your Wishbook

Practice introducing your Wishbook to your current or future partner (husband, girlfriend, etc). Share with them what you've realized would make you feel happy. Say the words out loud as if you are actually having the conversation.

Repeat the process until you feel comfortable asking for what you want and have a good feeling for what words you will use. The more you practice, the more confident you will be asking in real life. This can help you relax and feel more comfortable when you introduce your Wishbook to your loved one.

If you are in a relationship now, plan for some time in the near future to share your Wishbook with your partner. This can be a a great opportunity to reconnect and deepen your relationship.

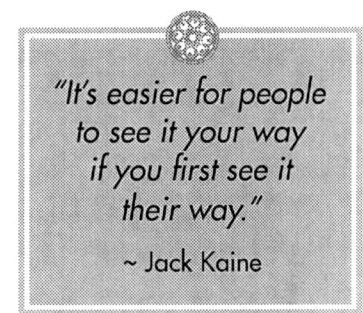

> *"It's easier for people to see it your way if you first see it their way."*
> ~ Jack Kaine

Choice & Compromise

Regardless of how committed you are to your requests, sometimes the person you are communicating with just isn't able, capable, or interested in doing things your way. So if this happens and the issue is still important to you, what do you do? Give up? Give in?

Start by considering a compromise. Work toward a solution that either feels comfortable for both parties or requires everyone to stretch equally toward middle ground. See if together you can resolve things in a way that honors your individual boundaries. Get creative. Consider anything that allows both of you to feel good about the end result. Dig deep and ask why. Occasionally what appears to be a motivating factor at the surface isn't the real reason behind your requests or the other person's refusal. The more you understand why each of you wants something, the easier it can be to determine how both of you can get your needs met.

Ultimately, compromise is a matter of perspective and priority. When you find yourself in conflict with someone you love, first stop and consider how important the issue is to you. Next, take a look at the amount of stress or strain that holding firm to your position can have on your relationship. Consider the big picture. How important is it that your do things your way? Follow your heart and do your best to choose what feels right to you.

Your ability to find compromise is an essential part of a sustainable and mutually respectful love relationship. So next time you want to spend a date doing something that your partner doesn't consider fun, offer a deal. If you both will agree to do it your way this time, then let your partner choose their perfect evening for your next date. Offering what you want now in trade for what they want later creates an equal exchange and is often an excellent way to come to agreement. Remember that compromising isn't a defeat. When you honor your boundaries and creatively find the common ground instead of remaining in conflict, your relationship wins.

> *"If you help others you will be helped, perhaps tomorrow, perhaps in 100 years, but you will be helped. Nature must pay off the debt. It is a mathematical law and all life is mathematics."*
>
> ~ Gurdjieff

> ### CIRCLE EXERCISE 4: Share Your Admiration
>
> Here is a chance to give everyone in the Circle the opportunity to learn about themselves and to celebrate their own successes from another person's perspective.
>
> 1. Have each group member write his or her own name on a folded piece of paper.
>
> 2. Place all the papers in a hat or bowl and have everyone pick one. Make sure that no has chosen their own name.
>
> 3. Next have the group stand or sit in a circle. One at a time, every member will share one or two things that they admire about the person they drew. Make sure all statements are positive.
>
> This is a great way to celebrate your experiences together.

And So You Have Come to the End

Congratulations! You have completed *More Love, More Joy!*. We hope this marks a new chapter in your personal life and creates a powerful difference in the future of your love relationships. Consider this your graduation. You have passed with flying colors and received the highest marks. Now nothing can stop you. So what's next?

Take Your Wishbook to the Next Level

The questions in this book are just the beginning. They provide a chance to explore the basics. If you want to take this work to the next level, contact us to learn more about our upcoming release, the *More Love, More Joy! Wishbook*. This workbook combines the contents of the original Wishbook from Chapter 8 along with an expanded list of questions and more detailed body maps. This new release will help you delve deeper into your relationship with both yourself and the one you love. It is a complete guide to help your partner understand you, your needs, and your desires while providing an opportunity to record your wishes in one concise journal.

Return as Often as You Wish

Review your Wishbook answers at least once a year and anytime you are in between relationships. This will help you stay aware of any new desires and add a fresh new dimension of ongoing communication in your relationship(s).

You may want to come back to this entire process again and again. Even on your second or third pass you may discover something you missed, gain a deeper sense of perspective, or develop a greater understanding or appreciation for yourself.

Join a Circle

If you've worked through this book on your own, you may still enjoy attending a *More Love, More Joy!* Circle. Whether or not you've already completed the process, doing this work as a part of a group can bring you new insight. Plus, the connections you'll make with Circle members can be enjoyable and fun.

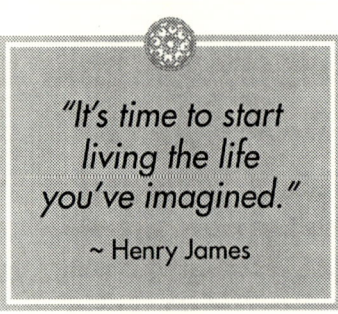

> *"It's time to start living the life you've imagined."*
> ~ Henry James

Become a Host

Would you be open to sharing with others your challenges and successes? If you would like to Host a Circle, we will provide you with free group outlines and promotional materials to help you get started. Just check our website for more information. It's a great way to support yourself and those in your Circle in getting more out of life.

Keep the Fire Alive

If you have found some part of what you learned during this process to be helpful, share your stories! Tell as many people as you can about what you discovered that was helpful and what you found really worked. Your history, your story, and your courage to ask for what you want can have the power to touch someone else's heart and reawaken their personal belief that they deserve to have the love they want, too.

More Love, More Joy! Gifts, Sponsorships, or Donations

If you would like to send this book, the meditation CD, or any products or services we offer as a gift, we can include a personalized card from you to the recipient. Sponsorships and gift certificates for *More Love, More Joy!* Seminars and other offerings can also be arranged.

All of our products and services can be given as gifts or donations to battered women's shelters, correctional facilities, recovery centers, and other approved non-profit organizations at discounted rates. If you would like help share this process by donating books, meditation CDs, or seminars, we will be happy to provide you with a list of groups who have requested gifts of our materials. Please contact our office to learn more about how you can spread more love and joy throughout the world.

Our Commitment

We are committed to doing our part to give back to the community. Ten percent (or more) of our net proceeds are donated to a variety of non-profit organizations. Additionally, we designate some of our time every year to share this process with individuals who might not otherwise be in a position to pay for our services. If you know of a non-profit group that would benefit from our work, we are always open to considering new sponsorships.

Please Keep in Touch

We hope you have enjoyed your journey. If you have found value doing the *More Love, More Joy!* process, we would love to hear about it. Nothing would bring us more pleasure than knowing that someone was inspired by this work. E-mail your personal stories, successes, and suggestions to feedback@MoreLoveMoreJoy.com.

If you are interested in learning more about this process or continuing the work you've started here, you can sign up for our mailing list, join us at one of our seminars, or schedule an appointment for one-on-one coaching. Check our website www.MoreLoveMoreJoy.com to connect with the *More Love, More Joy!* community and stay updated on any new developments.

Our Credo

- **Each of us is unique and ever evolving.**
  We are here to experience life at its fullest and to intimately know beauty, joy, and love. We are divinely good and worthy of love no matter what we do or have done in the past. We are open to believing that we are a part of something much bigger than just ourselves, even if we don't know what that is.

- **We always have choices in every aspect of our lives.**
  We each are responsible for our own emotions, our states of being, and all of our actions and experiences. We know that ultimately it is our choice to be happy and our responsibility to ask others for what we want.

- **Balance creates harmony.**
  We commit to loving others respectfully and based on the principle of equal exchange. We intend to release or bring balance to relationships where we give more than we receive or receive more than we give.

- **Love starts from within.**
  It is our ongoing intention to love ourselves, our bodies, our minds, our dreams, and our passions first and forever, even if no one else understands us. We intend to treat ourselves with love, kindness, and compassion everyday.

- **Our hearts always light the way.**
  We will speak our truths, act with integrity, and courageously follow our passions. We know we each are worthy of being loved in exactly the way we wish.

Index

A

Accepting generosity 108
Acknowledging 74–75
Action list 32, 33, 40, 61, 79, 101, 117, 133, 139
Aesop 109
Affirmations 22, 56, 62, 78, 100, 117
Agreement 91, 95, 100, 176
"And." *See* Conjunction "and"
Anniversaries 30, 31, 144–146
Apologizing 96–99
  how to apologize 97
  how to receive an apology 98
Appreciation 30, 93, 108, 109, 111, 178
Asking
  for help 39–40, 75, 78, 125
  for what you want 14, 16, 33, 38, 121, 131, 133, 135, 171, 172, 175, 178
  for what you want or something better 131, 133

B

Bach, Richard 28
Balance 13, 16, 18, 60, 68, 75, 89, 91, 93, 94, 112, 114, 117, 150, 180
Ball, Lucille 64

Benefit of the doubt 38
Best-case scenario 169
Birthdays 30, 31, 141–143
Black, Claudia 75
Body image. *See* Self talk
Body pleasure map 138, 160, 174
Boundaries 16, 51, 55, 56, 64, 65, 68, 75, 101, 121, 122, 125, 160, 173, 175, 176. *See also* Saying "no"
  honoring your 75
Buddha 58
Burnett, Carol 65
"But." *See* Conjunction "and"
  replacing with "and" 76

C

Carter-Scott, Cherie 15
Cather, Willa 137
Ceremony 91, 94
Chains (Karinthy) 132
Challenges 52, 178
Change 32, 33, 36, 44, 53, 54, 65, 73, 75, 92, 94, 119, 121, 122, 135, 138, 139
Choice 32, 53, 61, 75, 98, 104, 112, 180

choosing to be happy 53
freedom of 53
Circle 30, 134, 135, 154, 177
    discussions 49, 69, 87, 116
    exercises 22, 69, 177
    guidelines 24
    homework 23, 24, 26, 42, 62, 80, 102, 118, 136, 166
    hosts 24, 25, 178
    members 23, 25, 26, 42, 62, 80, 102, 118, 136, 166, 177
Clean Slate Meditation 45
Coffee press 89
Commitments 20, 33, 42, 61, 62, 80, 89, 102, 118, 136, 167
Communication 13, 16, 17, 22, 31, 32, 37, 54, 58, 74, 96, 111, 128, 150, 168, 169, 171, 173, 175
    importance of 37
    keeping your audience listening 37
    tips
        "I feel" messages 54–55
        "I love you" sandwich 169–173
        acknowledging 74, 75
        asking for help 39
        before an important conversation 169
        being a good receiver 111
        honoring your boundaries 75
        how to apologize 97–98
        how to receive an apology 98
        how to say "no" 75–76
        imagine the best possible outcome 169
        introducing your Wishbook to your partner 168, 173–174
        keep your "but" to yourself 76
        misunderstood messages 38–39
        preparing to ask for forgiveness 96
        respectfully disagreeing 77–78
        seeing the other person's perspective 96
        self-talk and self-respect 55–56
        send 'em love 169
        show your appreciation 111
        tone of voice 37–38
        value of a balanced apology 96

WIIFM 174
Compliment 104, 106, 108, 110, 111, 112, 114, 115, 170
Compromise 34, 175–176
Conjunction "and"
    diplomatically and respectfully disagreeing 77–78
    saying "no" 75–77
    usage 75–78
Contract 58, 59, 60, 61, 91, 94, 95
    karmic release 91
    to care for yourself with love 58
Couples 23, 126, 138, 173
    getting started 23
    introducing your Wishbook 173
    setting intentions together 126
Courage 12, 14, 28, 44, 45, 98, 124, 125, 178
Credo 21, 40–41, 180
Cutting the ties 91
The cycle of giving and receiving 106–108
The Cycle of Giving and Receiving Meditation 113–116

D

Dalai Lama 81
Desires 137
Disagreeing 77–78
Dreams 22, 41, 119, 131, 180
Dream Team 87–88, 101

E

Einstein, Albert
Emerson, Ralph Waldo 132
Emotions 22, 47, 86, 97, 167, 180
Energy flow
    illustrations 107
    of an accepted compliment 106–108
    of a rejected compliment 106–108
Equal exchange 13, 60, 111, 112, 115, 176, 180
Exercises 30, 32, 33, 35, 40, 50, 52, 55, 56, 57, 58, 65, 67, 69, 73, 76, 78, 79, 83, 87, 93, 100, 109, 112, 117,

Exercises (continued) 122, 125, 139, 160, 167, 171, 175, 177
Eye contact 74, 97, 105

F

Family 13, 24, 41, 44, 98, 109, 110, 119
Feelings 21, 32, 36, 38, 53, 55, 59, 66, 72, 84, 86, 91, 94, 96, 97, 98, 99, 100, 121, 125, 126, 127, 128, 169, 171, 172
Fight or flight 37
Follow your heart 45, 69
Forgiveness 81–101. *See also* releasing an emotionally charged relationship
  forgive others 88
  forgive yourself 83, 88, 93
Fortune 120, 121, 122, 123, 124, 135
Fortune cookie 120
Friends 31, 58, 134

G

Gandhi, Mahatma 11, 88
Generosity 108
  accepting 108
Gildwell, Jan 100
Giving 54, 96, 99, 103, 104, 105, 106, 108, 109, 110, 112, 114, 115, 116, 117, 122, 168, 191
Giving and receiving 96, 104, 106, 108, 114, 116, 117, 168
Goals 16, 21, 33, 37, 40, 61, 79, 82, 101, 117, 119, 124, 130, 131, 133, 134, 139, 191
Golden rule 92
Gratitude 128, 132, 169
Groups 22, 23, 24, 25, 87, 134, 135, 177, 178. *See also* Circles
Growth 79, 94, 138, 188, 190, 191
Guiding principles 74. *See also* Love rules
Gurdjieff 176

H

Habits 17, 65, 66, 67, 69
Hamilton, Eleanor 110
Happiness 13, 15, 16, 34, 48, 53, 57, 58,

Happiness (continued) 59, 60, 61, 73, 81, 87, 97, 105, 108, 116, 128, 129, 137, 138, 167, 168, 175, 179, 180, 191
  choosing to be happy 53
Harmony 60, 69, 71, 112, 180
Honoring receiving 18, 106, 110, 116, 117
Honoring your boundaries 75. *See also* Boundaries; *See also* Saying "no"
Host 24, 25, 178

I

I'm sorry 39, 96, 97, 98, 100, 101. *See also* Apologizing
"I feel" messages 54, 55, 61
I honor receiving 110
"I love you" sandwich 169, 170, 171, 172, 173
Imagine the best possible outcome 169
Inner conflict 75
Inner peace 75
Intentions 19, 94, 124, 125, 126, 131
  consciously setting 124
  setting intentions as a couple 126
  stating your 125
  supercharge your 126
Intimacy 16, 121, 156

J

James, Henry 178
Journal 22, 32, 35, 36, 52, 65, 67, 68, 93, 116, 136, 137, 177. *See also* Supply list

K

Kaine, Jack 175
Karinthy, Frigyes 132
Karma 91, 92, 94, 95
  karmic debts 92, 95
  karmic release contract 95
  karmic ties 95
  primer 92
Kindness 58, 73, 74, 86, 87, 92, 104, 109, 111, 115, 116, 138, 180

184 MORE LOVE, MORE JOY!

Kipling, Rudyard 138

L

Labels 46, 47, 49
Learning to receive 105
Letting Go of Limiting Beliefs Meditation 126-129
Letting go of the past 81. *See also* Releasing
Limiting beliefs 126
Listening 20, 37, 38, 51, 54, 74, 75, 97, 98, 151, 170, 174
  keeping your audience 37. *See also* Communication
Love 13, 14, 15, 16, 17, 18, 19, 20, 21, 23, 24, 25, 26, 30, 31, 33, 40, 41, 42, 43, 45, 53, 58, 62, 63, 64, 65, 67, 70, 73, 74, 79, 80, 93, 102, 117, 118, 119, 133, 136, 153, 166, 169, 170, 171, 172, 173, 177, 178, 179, 180, 182, 184, 186, 187, 188, 189, 190
  love life 13, 16, 17, 18, 29, 35, 36, 41, 65, 92, 119, 121, 124, 125, 137, 138, 167
  love life inventory 30, 31
  poster 41, 62, 102
  relationship 13, 14, 16, 17, 37, 43, 96, 112, 167, 176
  role models 18, 66, 67, 68, 69, 71, 72, 73, 79
  rules 69, 71, 73
  self-love 16, 67, 71, 84

M

Manifestation 119, 125, 126, 131
Meditations 21, 42, 45, 49, 62, 70, 80, 83, 87, 102, 113, 116, 118, 126, 187, 189
  Chapter 3 - Clean Slate 45-49
  Chapter 4 - Releasing Other's Rules About Love 70-73
  Chapter 5 - Self-Forgiveness 83-87
  Chapter 6 - The Cycle of Giving and Receiving 113-116
  Chapter 7- Letting Go of Limiting Beliefs 126-129
Members 23, 25, 26, 42, 62, 80, 102, 118, 136, 166, 177. *See also* Circles
Miracle Networking 118, 133-135
  gathering 118, 134-135
Misunderstood messages 38-39
More Love, More Joy! Circles. *See* Circles
Motivation 33

N

Nidetch, Jean 104
Nin, Anais 99
Notebook 65, 67, 117

O

O'Neill, Edmund 56
Overcoming your obstacles 33

P

Past
  letting go of the 81. *See also* Releasing
Patterns 12, 17, 65, 66, 67, 69, 92, 122. *See also* Habits; *See also* Karma
Peer groups. *See* Circles; *See also* Groups
Personal needs 58
Perspective 18, 75, 92, 96, 174, 176, 177, 178
  change your 75
  seeing other person's 96
Peters, Tom 97
Post meditation 49, 87, 116
Practice 55, 61, 76, 87, 101, 171, 175
Priorities 18, 33, 75
Proust, Marcel 103

R

Ralph Waldo Emerson 132
Receiving
  being a good receiver 111
  learning to receive 105, 109
  log 109
Rejection 106
Relationships 12, 13, 14, 15, 16, 17, 18,

Relationships (continued) 19, 22, 30, 32, 33, 34, 37, 38, 39, 40, 43, 54, 60, 63, 64, 65, 67, 78, 79, 90, 91, 92, 93, 95, 96, 97, 98, 99, 105, 110, 112, 126, 131, 137, 138, 167, 168, 169, 170, 171, 172, 173, 174, 175, 176, 177, 178, 180
  goals 33, 40
Releasing
  "love rules" you no longer want 69–73
  an emotionally charged relationship 93–94
  limiting beliefs 126
  patterns 12, 17, 65
Releasing Others' Rules About Love Meditation 70–73
Requesting action 54. *See also* Communication
Requests 20, 24, 38, 75, 76, 78, 135, 139, 140, 145, 170, 174, 175, 176
Respect 13, 16, 30, 55, 56, 58, 59, 68, 74, 88, 111, 122, 171
Respectfully disagreeing 77–78
Roberts, Donna 23
Role models 18, 66, 67, 68, 69, 71, 72, 73, 79
Romance 27, 28, 35, 43, 65, 122
  romantic love 65
  romantic relationship 43, 63, 131
Roosevelt, Eleanor 44
Ross, Percy 167
Rules 18, 69, 70, 73, 74
  circle guidelines 24–25
  contract to care for yourself with love 58
  love rules 18, 69, 71, 73, 74

S

Salzberg, Sharon 124
Saying "I'm sorry" 96–101. *See also* Apologizing; *See also* Communication
Saying "no" 75–77. *See also* Boundaries; *See also* Conjunction "and"; *See also* Communication

Self
  care 58–60
  forgiveness ritual 89
  respect 55, 55–56
  talk 55–56, 58
Self-Forgiveness Meditation 83–87
Send 'em love 169
Sex 31, 156–159. *See also* Body pleasure map
Something wonderful 57, 61, 79, 101, 115, 117, 133, 139
Staying motivated 40
Stein, Ben 27
Success 25, 134, 135, 177, 178, 179
Supply list 20
Support 14, 19, 23, 25, 37, 39, 126, 150, 172, 178, 179, 188, 190

T

Thank you 40, 79, 94, 95, 108, 110, 111, 112, 114, 115
  being a good receiver 111–112
  show your appreciation 111
Tip of the week 41, 61, 79, 101, 117, 133, 139
Tone of voice 37–38
Tooting your own horn 52
Transformation 46, 79, 85
Trust 15, 59, 63, 67, 72, 97, 172

U

Universal balance 112

W

Ward, William Arthur 119
Weekly commitments 33, 42, 61, 62, 79, 80, 101, 102, 117, 118, 133, 136, 139
What you want 14, 16, 22, 27, 29, 32, 33, 36, 38, 39, 54, 74, 97, 121, 122, 125, 126, 128, 131, 132, 133, 135, 140, 169, 171, 172, 173, 174, 175, 176, 178
WIIFM 174
Wilde, Oscar 43

Winfrey, Oprah 52
Wishbook 17, 19, 20, 21, 136, 137, 138, 139, 141, 166, 168, 173, 174, 175, 177, 178. *See also* Body pleasure map
  building your 137–165
  introducing your 173–175
  making your personal 139–159
  practice sharing your 175
Wishes 135, 137, 138, 168, 171, 177
Wolfgang von Goethe, Johann 63

Quick Order Form

	Price	Qty.	Total
More Love, More Joy! (Book)	$14.95		
More Love, More Joy! Meditations (CD)	$14.95		
More Love, More Joy! Combo Set: 1 Book + 1 Meditation CD Note: Count Each Set as 1 Item for Shipping	$24.95 (Save $5.00)		
More Love, More Joy! Group Bundle: 10 Books + 1 Meditation CD Note: Shipping for Each Group Bundle is $8.95	$124.95 (Save $39.50)		
U.S. Shipping/Handling for First Item	$4.60 ($8.95 ea. for Group Bundles)		
U.S. S/H for Each Additional Item (See notes above for Sets/Bundles)	$2.25		

Call for international and expedited shipping rates. See our website, www.MoreLoveMoreJoy.com, for a complete list of products and services.

Subtotal: _____

Sales Tax (for WA State Shipments Only) Add 8.4%

Total: _____

Please Print Clearly:

Name: _____

Ship to Address: _____

City: _____ State: _____ Zip: _____

E-mail Address: _____

Phone Number: (_____) _____ — _____

Payment Enclosed: ☐ Check # _____ ☐ Visa ☐ Mastercard

Credit Card #: _____ — _____ — _____ — _____

Expires: _____ /20_____ Security Code on Back of Card (3 Digits): _____

Name on Card: _____

Billing Street Number: _____ Billing Zip Code: _____

Signature: _____ Date: _____

Send me FREE info on: ☐ Other Books ☐ Seminars ☐ Personal Coaching

PLEASE SEE REVERSE SIDE FOR ADDITIONAL ORDERING INFORMATION
DISCOVERY BAY BOOKS • Phone: 800-936-0036 • Fax: 360-379-1964

Submit Your Order

MAIL:
DISCOVERY BAY BOOKS
2023 E. Sims Way #275
Port Townsend, WA 98368

PHONE: 360-379-1960

TOLL-FREE: 800-936-0036

FAX: 360-379-1964

ONLINE: www.MoreLoveMoreJoy.com

Make Checks Payable to:
Discovery Bay Books

Satisfaction Guaranteed:
We offer hassle-free returns. If your purchase does not meet your expectations, return your merchandise in unopened, like-new condition within 30 days for a full refund, less any amount paid for shipping and handling. Call our office for a Return Merchandise Authorization Number and more information.

Full List of Products & Services Available Online:
This order form includes just a small portion of our *More Love, More Joy!* offerings. Online you will find more information and will be able to order all of our *More Love, More Joy!* products and services including gift certificates for merchandise, seminars, and personal coaching. Give the gift of *More Love, More Joy!* to everyone on your list! Visit www.MoreLoveMoreJoy.com today!

About Discovery Bay Books
Discovery Bay Books is an independent publisher focused on bringing books to the world that support personal and professional growth, inspiration, and discovery. Ten percent or more of our profits are donated to charity every year.

Quick Order Form

	Price	Qty.	Total
More Love, More Joy! (Book)	$14.95		
More Love, More Joy! Meditations (CD)	$14.95		
More Love, More Joy! Combo Set: 1 Book + 1 Meditation CD Note: Count Each Set as 1 Item for Shipping	$24.95 (Save $5.00)		
More Love, More Joy! Group Bundle: 10 Books + 1 Meditation CD Note: Shipping for Each Group Bundle is $8.95	$124.95 (Save $39.50)		
U.S. Shipping/Handling for First Item	$4.60 ($8.95 ea. for Group Bundles)		
U.S. S/H for Each Additional Item See notes above for Sets/Bundles	$2.25		

Call for international and expedited shipping rates. See our website, www.MoreLoveMoreJoy.com, for a complete list of products and services.

Subtotal: _____

Sales Tax (for WA State Shipments Only) Add 8.4% _____

Total: _____

Please Print Clearly:

Name: _____

Ship to Address: _____

City: _____ State: _____ Zip: _____

E-mail Address: _____

Phone Number: (_____) _____ — _____

Payment Enclosed: ❑ Check # _____ ❑ Visa ❑ Mastercard

Credit Card #: _____ — _____ — _____ — _____

Expires: _____ /20_____ Security Code on Back of Card (3 Digits): _____

Name on Card: _____

Billing Street Number: _____ Billing Zip Code: _____

Signature: _____ Date: _____

Send me FREE info on: ❑ Other Books ❑ Seminars ❑ Personal Coaching

PLEASE SEE REVERSE SIDE FOR ADDITIONAL ORDERING INFORMATION
DISCOVERY BAY BOOKS • Phone: 800-936-0036 • Fax: 360-379-1964

Submit Your Order

MAIL:
DISCOVERY BAY BOOKS
2023 E. Sims Way #275
Port Townsend, WA 98368

PHONE: 360-379-1960

TOLL-FREE: 800-936-0036

FAX: 360-379-1964

ONLINE: www.MoreLoveMoreJoy.com

Make Checks Payable to:
Discovery Bay Books

Satisfaction Guaranteed:
We offer hassle-free returns. If your purchase does not meet your expectations, return your merchandise in unopened, like-new condition within 30 days for a full refund, less any amount paid for shipping and handling. Call our office for a Return Merchandise Authorization Number and more information.

Full List of Products & Services Available Online:
This order form includes just a small portion of our *More Love, More Joy!* offerings. Online you will find more information and will be able to order all of our *More Love, More Joy!* products and services including gift certificates for merchandise, seminars, and personal coaching. Give the gift of *More Love, More Joy!* to everyone on your list! Visit www.MoreLoveMoreJoy.com today!

About Discovery Bay Books
Discovery Bay Books is an independent publisher focused on bringing books to the world that support personal and professional growth, inspiration, and discovery. Ten percent or more of our profits are donated to charity every year.

About the Authors

Jennifer Martin:
Jennifer's experience includes working as a business consultant, personal coach, and certified hypnotherapist. Nothing brings her more pleasure than helping people discover their own potential for happiness and financial success, while creating lives they love. Jennifer has been giving seminars for more than 12 years and has led various networking and personal growth groups in California, Oregon, and Washington. Currently residing in Port Townsend, WA, she lives in her dream house with her partner of 10 years. Jennifer enjoys spending time gardening, thrift store shopping, hanging out with friends, and eating ice cream.

Ryan West:
Ryan has been helping people discover how to achieve their goals for many years. Having owned her own marketing and graphic design company, she has a history of crafting messages to help her clients discover success in any area they endeavor. Originally from Wisconsin, Ryan now makes her home in Port Townsend, WA. She has been romantically involved with the "love of her life" for nearly a decade. In her spare time she enjoys traveling, going out for dinner, doing home makeover projects, shopping online, and doing internet research.

Printed in the United States
200176BV00010B/1-30/A